This book combines first hand testimony to the power of God in creation and the revelation of God in Scripture. The hand of God revealed in what He has made and the heart of God revealed in what He has said. Martin takes us on his personal journey in a way that invites us to join him in the growing discovery of the goodness of God.

STEPHEN GAUKROGER
Director/Founder of Clarion Trust International

In a remarkable blend of Scripture, personal experience and devotional style, Martin C. Haworth journeys through the awe inspiring wonder and grandeur of the Scottish hills to the glory and honour of the Creator of all things. Every chapter opens up a new perspective on the realities of life as one man comes to know and understand the saving grace of his Creator God.

WAYNE SUTTON
Senior Pastor, Carrubbers Christian Centre, Edinburgh

Most hill walkers and mountaineers appreciate that there is more to the experience than reaching the summit and enjoying the view. It is quite clear to me that there is a spiritual element to our enjoyment of the mountains. *A Clearing of the Mists* does exactly what it says on the tin! It helps us navigate through a number of spiritual themes brought to life by the experiences of the author as he climbs the mountains of Scotland. This is not a guidebook to a few Munros, it is a guidebook to understanding our spiritual journey through life with notes and practical instructions to help us meditate on our own experiences.

MIKE PESCOD
Abacus Mountaineering and
Chairman, Fort William Mountain Festival, Fort William

A
CLEARING
OF THE
MISTS

IN PURSUIT OF WISDOM
UPON THE SCOTTISH HILLS

MARTIN C. HAWORTH

CHRISTIAN
FOCUS

Cover image used by permission of Scott Robertson Landscape Photography (www.flickr.com/photos/roksoff).

Buachaille Etive Mor, Glencoe is one of Scotland's most iconic mountains. Scott Robertson captured this classic autumn scene from Beinn a' Chrulaiste, the mountain opposite The Buachaille Etive Mor range.

Copyright © @ Martin C. Haworth 2016

paperback ISBN 978-1-78191-718-3
epub ISBN 978-1-78191-735-0
mobi ISBN 978-1-78191-736-7

10 9 8 7 6 5 4 3 2 1

Published in 2016
by
Christian Focus Publications Ltd,
Geanies House, Fearn, Ross-shire,
IV20 1TW, Great Britain.

www.christianfocus.com

Cover design by Daniel Van Straaten

Printed and bound
by
Bell & Bain, Glasgow

MIX
Paper from
responsible sources
FSC® C007785

Contents

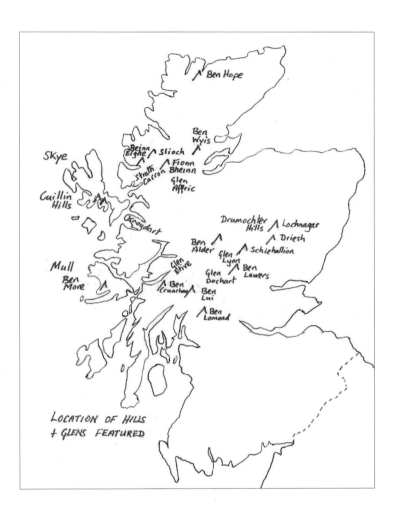

Ben Hope

Ben Wyis

Beinn Eighe · Slioch

Skye

Strath Carron · Fionn Bheinn

Glen Affric

Cuillin Hills

Knoydart

Drumochter Hills · Lochnagar

· Driesh

Ben Alder · Glen Lyon · Schiehallion

Mull

Glen Etive

Ben More

Glen Dochart · Ben Lawers

· Ben Cruachan · Ben Lui

· Ben Lomond

LOCATION OF HILLS + GLENS FEATURED

7

List of maps
(page numbers of where they appear)

The Higher Way

Seek the inspired way
Ascending the distant heights;
Be almost heedless of care,
Deaf to the clamouring caution –
If you heed you'll not travel far,
Never to leave the crowd.

Face the fear others impose.
Be bold – do step out of line!
Break from the unremarkable rank
Marching all so unspectacularly
To the dreary drum down the highway,
Taking the short, the expedient line
Gathering the honours, the dues of duty
Marking some slow death in a rut.
Don't tarry with those who gave up
Be deaf to their 'now-we-know-better!'

At the fork in the way do more than pause,
Take time to ponder the steps that led here.
Take courage for the way ahead.
Strive for the heights,
Dare tread the driven snow;
Don't linger long indecisive
For the moment passes when choice flees.

With all your might, make for the distant border,
Muster all courage, yield to the Spirit
Set your sight on the far horizon
To immense vistas of sun-blessed summits.
Press on before clouds descend
And night brings regret
Of the higher way never taken.

Martin C. Haworth

9

Acknowledgements

I'm grateful to fellow Munroist, Iain K. Macleod, for all his interaction with this text and yet with whom I've never climbed.

Dedication

I dedicate this to my wife – Alexandra – for her patience and understanding in helping me make the round of the Munros; to my children, Iain and Hannah, for their companionship on the few memorable outings shared together and to my own father who inspired me to make for the heights.

Good Riddance:

to the pair of state-of-the-art trousers that chafed me on so many climbs.

Preface

The fear of the Lord is the beginning of wisdom
And the knowledge of the Holy One is understanding.
(Prov. 9:10)

Many who climb the Munros eclipse me in terms of speed and daring and epic exploits. I can make no boast and in no way do I put myself forward as some luminary of the hills. With the passing of youth, I dispensed with competing against the clock in walking a round of summits. In taking out the competitive edge, I learned to slow, to stop, to look about; to slowly absorb and to be absorbed. Hills can humble, forcing us to turn back, or if reaching their peak, can remind us we're only flesh and blood when acknowledging a limp in our step en route back to the car. This isn't an account that celebrates the virtues of this hill and that route for there are already plenty of good accounts and guides. I didn't take to the hills because there were Munros, for the challenge of ascending 282 summits of 3,000 feet plus. Like several Munroists, I have baulked at ticking off completed Munros from the list as though they were conquered and of no further consequence other than the names of trophies. To reduce the motive of spending a day in the hills to ticking off the summit's name from a list seems sacrosanct. And yet, I cannot deny the undoubted sense of achievement to climb every peak along a ridge and to walk most ridges within a region. And so paradoxically I, too, admit to the thrill of adding to the quota, of subtracting from the tally of those yet to be done!

But if it's some arithmetic obsession driving us on, then we're missing the point, desensitised to what can be learned from the hills. The hills beckon with their call to the wild, to reconnect with that primeval state of being the wanderer, drawn by the curious lure of what lies beyond the horizon, inspiring something of the heroic as you battle with the onslaught of elemental forces and have to walk further than ever before.

I was drawn to the wild places for connection with something pure and great. I went in search of transcendence: when our spirit is lifted beyond the natural realm to perceive something of heavenly realities, even of God Himself. It would be helpful to expand on what I mean by 'transcendence'. The Cambridge Dictionary defines the root 'transcend' as: 'to go further, rise above, or be more important or better than something, especially a limit.' Taking the concept of going beyond a limit, I use transcendence to describe the sense of going beyond the physical satisfaction of climbing a hill, that the taking to the hills isn't only for the purpose of reaching the summit to see magnificent panoramas of wild mountainous landscapes. These are the outward trappings that have value in themselves, creating a sense of well-being, of accomplishment, and that is where the natural limit is set and for some hillwalkers this is the goal of their quest.

However, what exceeds that experience is perhaps more easily understood if I were to use a musical analogy. At the basic level the ear appreciates the sound, inspiring emotions such as a sense of calm or happiness, and leading to a connection with the musician/composer. What transcends this is when our spirits are strangely moved and gain a momentary glimpse into something that is profound and hard to articulate. It's these moments of spine-tingling perception that mysteriously touch, which communicate something intrinsically important of what it is to be essentially human; a spiritual experience that tells us that we're not alone.

Some people experience the same when in the hills, of suddenly being caught up by some force outside of themselves. It isn't the culmination of appreciating a view that produces 'fine feelings'. Our spirit tangibly recognises something pure and holy and exceedingly great. It can leave us with a sense of extraordinary wonder. It is as if for a moment we have popped our gaze outside the bubble of the material world and for a second perceived something that is awesome and matters very much, if only we could determine what it is.

I hope many readers will identify with such spiritual glimpses and see how God can communicate to us through these transcendent moments. The nature imagery of the Bible often illustrates the desire for knowledge and understanding that resonates with those in awe of nature's grandeur, leading us to consider the big themes of life, appealing for vision and courage to enlarge our goals. The desire to make for the summit is a metaphor for the human quest for transcendence, the search for wisdom when in our honest moments alone in the hills we seek to make sense of our lives and in the process we can glimpse the Creator who is not only all-wise, but one who seeks *us*. Attitudes are challenged, characters formed as fears are faced, when trials demand perseverance, where defeat tempers success and keeps us humble and in awe.

I also want to impart how hillcraft translates into shaping life skills and attitudes which in turn can affect our spiritual formation. Taking to the hills has been a pursuit to know God's guidance and discipline and is why I most often go without other companions. A day alone in the hills gives a different take on circumstances; changes priorities or makes me relinquish the secondary to focus more on what is of consequence.

I have incorporated an autobiographical thread which follows some chronology, tracing the spiritual developments towards discovering a Christian faith. I have tried to be true to the way I saw things at the time in the hope that this might resonate with those who don't have a Christian perspective as well as to provide understanding for those who read this from a Christian viewpoint.

For the sake of starting my story, I was born and brought up on the outskirts of Manchester which being confined in a crowded and uninspiring place perhaps partly explains my love for the wild places. As my father grew a love for the hills in me, I am glad that my children, Iain and Hannah, have likewise cultivated that same wonder of nature and have an adventurous spirit. My wife, Alexandra, values nature too, but leaves it to the rest of the family to get wet and blown about upon the heights. Manchester now feels a long time ago and Scotland has been my home since 1976 albeit with two stints of working abroad amounting to fourteen years away. Scotland became the birthplace of our children whose births were registered in the wool shop in Dunkeld. Scotland is dear to my heart, especially the Highlands and its people.

Introduction on how to use the guided meditations

At the end of each chapter are meditations and suggestions to help explore your own memories and to encourage fresh perspective and experience as you gather your own defining moments that shape and strengthen faith. They are intended to encourage a prayerful response. I hope these will be useful meditations to help you on your own personal journey as we travel the Munros together.

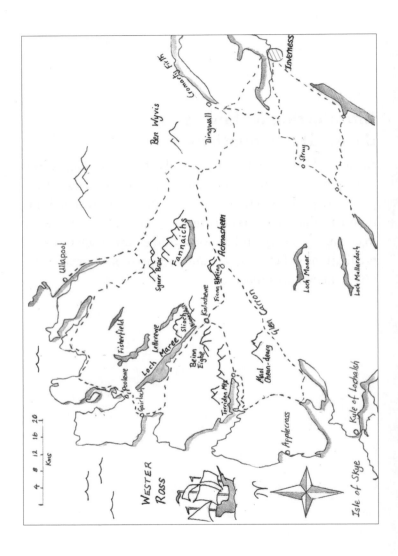

1

Exquisite Beauty and Mystery

Glen Carron and Ben Hope

ARRIVING in Glen Carron (see 'Wester Ross' map, p. 16) in late September, I switched off the car headlights, my eyes taking time to adjust to the moonlight. I could make out the hills about me in solid, bold silhouettes against the slightly translucent black of the night sky. The starry night views were so splendid that I left the warmth and comfort of the car to stand in awe of the majesty rising around me like a crescendo of praise.

Majesty

The heavens declare the glory of God; the skies proclaim the work of his hands.

Day after day they pour forth speech; night after night they display knowledge.

There is no speech or language where their voice is not heard.

Their voice goes out into all the earth, their words to the ends of the world. (Ps. 19:1-4)

Scenes bathed in moonlight are captivating, and hiding all the intricate details, present more of an impression, suggesting vague outlines of wood and field. I was intrigued to see something like snow up in the high corrie and had wondered whether the first flakes of a new winter had fallen. But with it looking 'like snow' it gave me pause to doubt and yet I couldn't think what else it could be with just that level of light, leaving me puzzling again and again. Eventually I went to sleep, but as in the manner of sleeping in the car, I periodically awoke and peered bleary-eyed, intrigued, up towards the high corrie, still wondering. My attention was captivated by the brilliance of the heavens with vast clusters of stars rare to be seen in such profusion that I was left in awe and worship of the Creator. The skies really were proclaiming the work of His hands.

The sense of immensity of the universe on a very clear night makes you feel miniscule, in total awe of the magnitude of space, the ageless stars making a human lifespan feel so very finite, of such brevity as to be totally insignificant if plotted on an infinite timeline. To be alone under such a sky is to feel truly inconsequential and puts all of man's proud achievements into perspective:

> *when I consider your heavens, the work of your fingers,*
> *the moon and stars, which you have set in place,*
> *what is man that you are mindful of him*
> *the son of man that you care for him?*   (Ps. 8:3-4 NIV)

Creation is there to enthral. We should be in raptures and profoundly feel its mysteries. Although made in God's image, we are products of His creation as God reminds Job:

Can you bind the beautiful Pleiades?
Can you loose the cords of Orion?
Can you bring forth the constellations in their seasons
Or lead out the Bear with its cubs?
Do you know the laws of the heavens?
Can you set up God's dominion over the earth?
    (Job 38:31-33)

How fleeting a thing it is to be human and yet within the soul there is a longing for permanence – 'He has also set eternity in the hearts of men, yet they cannot fathom what God has done from beginning to end' (Eccles. 3:11). Forever there's been a deep desire to vault above the tragedy of death, to attain an unending sense of being, to belong to something higher and of enduring quality that knows no decay nor end. Such a sky awakens these very longings and for some inspires praise for the Maker, one who made us and filled us with immortal aspirations as a consequence of being made in God's own image.

When morning dawned, the light on the corrie revealed a light-coloured scree that had looked whiter still in the moonlight and had so softened and blurred its hard edges as to give it the appearance of a smooth sheet of snow. Moonlight certainly brings a poetic quality to the common things of day, making night vistas worth seeing in spite of the chill and inconvenience of the hour.

I discovered late in life the joy of winter hillwalking, taken up out of a sense of despair of how few outings could be mustered over the sparse summer of the north. With the end in sight to complete 200 Munros, it hastened my pace, giving fresh impetus to complete the glorious round.

A late winter ascent of Maol Chean-dearg above Glen Carron was memorable for the views of the Torridon Mountains from its summit and for the crazy descent down a snow shoot from near its peak. Normally being a solo walker made me aware of the precariousness of my situation. Whether it was tiredness after a tediously steep ascent, or the sudden impulse to throw caution to the wind I don't know, but before I properly took stock, I removed my plastic survival bag from my small backpack and unfolding a section the size of a toboggan, I sat down and went careering down a narrow and steep gulley before digging in my heels when fear dictated. At least I knew

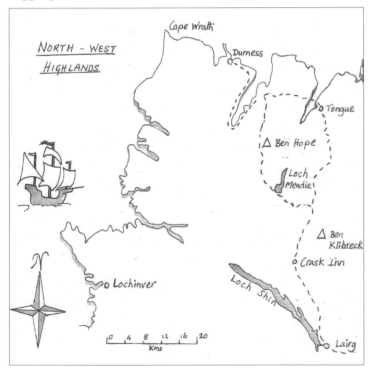

there was no sudden cliff drop as I had earlier painstakingly wended my way up this very route. It was exhilarating to recklessly speed on down, sometimes bruised over the tops of boulders or wayside debris, and I whooped and laughed. It did no good to my survival bag but gave me great joy.

Ben Hope (see 'North West Highlands' map, p. 20) – the most northerly Munro – was likewise tackled in the winter. The evening before I had dined at the Crask Inn on a selection of fowl a French party, the only other occupants in the inn, had shot earlier in the day, singing raptures about the game. The Crask Inn is wonderfully unpretentious, a place resisting the urge to modernise, with its stone-flagged floors and simple bar left unattended when the owner takes feed out to the sheep on the hill. When he returned he placed muddy boots beside the hearth and hung his waterproofs from a beam above the fire making a pool on the flags below that shortly began to steam away to nothingness.

Star display

That night I spent in the car up on the pass above the inn, on the flanks of Ben Klibreck, the car thermometer read eight below zero. The constellations spread out so numerous and breathtaking that it was hard to close my eyes, not for the cold, but for the sheer brilliance of the heavens. What a gift – relishing this wonderful display all on my own, a spectacle it seemed for a private audience. With every chilly awakening the huge constellations had shifted, seemingly wheeling about the naked heavens on some colossal axis. It was hauntingly beautiful, making one thirst for knowledge of the stars, to know their shapes and position. It seems that our Neolithic forefathers who raised immense stone circles in alignment with solstices were in awe of the celestial bodies, noting how the sun and the moon interconnected with seasons and fruitfulness, guiding their agricultural cycle. Such knowledge mingled with much mystery kept those ancient ancestors from arrogance and held them in awe of something far greater than their human endeavours and led them to worship. The Babylonians and the Greeks were intimately acquainted with the stars, drawn by wonder, keen to discern their mystery because they were acutely aware of the night skies under which they ate and talked, loved and died. We, in our brightly lit cities, have so far alienated ourselves from the night skies that most of us are pretty clueless about constellations. The familiar knowledge of the stars known to ancient laymen has become the specialised field of the astronomer.

Shout to the Lord

The next morning was extremely crisp – the lower-lying regions of earth remained ashen and moribund as yet untouched by the dawn light. Three voluminous columns of cloud rose vertically above the frozen scenes in a strange fashion that caught the eye. Dawn touched these columns, suffused them with a pale pink to match the snowy peaks, which rose resplendent in search of the light. Dawns are often unremarkable but this one was an exception – it brought the world alive with gladness and made you want to sing to the Lord.

> *I will sing and make music with all my soul,*
> *Awake, harp and lyre! I will awaken the dawn.*
> *I will praise you, O LORD, among the nations;*
> *I will sing praises of you among the peoples.*

For great is your love, higher than the heavens;
Your faithfulness reaches to the skies.
Be exalted, O God, above the heavens,
And let your glory be over all the earth.　(Ps. 108:1-5)

The reference to 'Awake, harp and lyre! I will awaken the dawn', makes me recall the songwriter Noel Richards, who referring to his own habit of taking 'quiet times' dismissed the term, asserting that these should be 'noisy times', as he so enjoyed starting the day singing to the Lord. How the Lord must delight in the exuberance of His children. I am sure hearing the first utterances of 'Good Morning Lord' from the awakening Buhid tribal folk of Mindoro in the Philippines, whom we used to live with, warmed His heart just as much as our hearts were warmed when we heard our toddler calling out from his cot, 'Morning, Eesh!' – Eesh being his pronunciation of Jesus.

Loch Meadie was all iced over and the huge herds of deer that had ventured down to the road seeking food, licked the salt from the tarmac. The dawn light intensifying upon the tops of the peaks flushed them with a deep orange pink, vibrant against the ice-blue skies and gave this dawn an exotic air, bringing to mind the opening stanza of *The Rubáiyát of Omar Khayyám* as translated by Edward FitzGerald:

Awake! for Morning in the Bowl of Night
Has flung the Stone that puts the Stars to Flight:
And Lo! the Hunter of the East has caught
The Sultán's Turret in a Noose of Light.

Leaving the warmth of the car for the rawness of that early morning chill was challenging. My legs were reluctant to get

23

into their stride on the sudden steep rise of Ben Hope, but the winter land enthralled. Where the heather grew longer, snow, wind and ice had created much more substantial heather shapes like lumps of bleached coral. Up on the high ridge, wind and chill had left delicate traceries on the surface of the snow, rather like the scallop edges left in the sand at the sea's edge. The summit dome was windswept, so much so that only a thin layer of snow remained upon which the frost raised delicate motifs, large and shiny like crystal stones, fused with filigrees of frost. The concrete summit cairn was quite transformed with snow and ice crystals, and having been 'stretched' horizontally by a raging wind, looked magnificent in the winter sun like an art nouveau sculpture.

Miniature wonders

These were unexpected delights I had never seen before, their rarity making them all the more special. It's easy to miss these miniature wonders if the mountain seems off-limits in the grip of winter or early in the morning, when caution would keep you down in the glen. And I believe that is a metaphor for choices in life. Perhaps too much caution keeps us from ascending the heights and revelling in something rare and more wonderful. It can be our own indolence, our love for ease and comfort, or opting for what is predictable that keeps us from scaling the exalted ridges that transcend high above the turbid flow of life.

> *He made the earth by his power;*
> *He founded the world by his wisdom*
> *And stretched out the heavens by his understanding.*
>   (Jer. 51:15)

24

Wasn't I glad I spent freezing nights in a car so that I could see afresh the heavens stretched out by His understanding.

MEDITATION & SUGGESTIONS

'Night sky'

Part of the theme of this chapter is about opening our eyes to the wonder of the stars, the magnitude of the universe that leads to wonder and to reflect on the brevity and seeming insignificance of our passing, a speck of time in eternity.

Look out for a clear night sky and drive out into the country for a night-time stroll to marvel at the stars. You can check out the immediate weather forecast as it is presented on an hour by hour prediction on the weather website: http://www.bbc.co.uk/weather – keying in your specific location.

Feel the immensity of the night sky and how miniscule our mortal lives are in comparison. It's rather sobering. Isn't it amazing that this magnificent God of the whole universe is mindful of us. Read Psalm 19:1-4 and Psalm 8:3-4 (quoted in this chapter) as you contemplate the heavens and consider too these verses:

He who made the Pleiades and Orion,
Who turns blackness into dawn
And darkens day into night,
Who calls for the waters of the sea
And pours them out over the face of the land –
The Lord is his name.   (Amos 5:8)

He spreads out the northern skies over empty space;
He suspends the earth over nothing.
He wraps up the waters in his clouds,
Yet the clouds do not burst under their weight.
He covers the face of the full moon,
Spreading his clouds over it.
He marks out the horizon on the face of the waters
For a boundary between light and darkness.
    (Job 26:7-10)

These are not scientific observations of the heavens, but they are full of wonder and adoration for the One who made them. A modern scientific mind remarked:

The fairest thing we can experience is the mysterious. … He who knows it not and can no longer wonder, no longer feel amazement, is as good as dead, a snuffed-out candle.   ALBERT EINSTEIN

Taking up this theme of wonder that leads us to worship, Warren Wiersbe commented:

Wonder and worship go together and worship leads to depth. Wonder and worship help us put daily life into perspective, and perspective helps us determine our values. This may explain why modern society wants entertainment instead of enrichment, and a good time rather than a good life.

Our spirits long for eternity which the night skies inspire. For the believer there is the expectation of a new body, far more splendid than our current one, that will not experience illness or decay. In view of this do you honestly still fear death? Bring your concerns or praise to the Lord – be assured of His greatness that the sky above suggests. If you do not share this faith, consider God's heavenly revelation through the stars, of how we are part of something vast and mind-blowing. Reconsider the psalmist's thoughts, 'What is man that you are mindful of him, the son of man that you care for him?' (Ps. 8:4). This declares that God does know of your existence – He created you – and He knows and is concerned for you. In Psalm 139:13-16, it is more explicit, 'You created my inmost being; you knit me together in my mother's womb. I praise you because I am fearfully and wonderfully made … My frame was not hidden from you when I was made in the secret place, when I was woven together in the depths of the earth, your eyes saw my unformed body.'

Sunrise/Sunset

Make an 'appointment' to watch a sunrise/sunset. Try to be intentional about this – check the aforementioned website to note the time of sunrise/sunset. Currently in early February in Central Scotland, every sunrise averages out at about two minutes earlier every morning and every sunset two minutes later than the previous day and so be encouraged to combat the winter blues by noting the days lengthening approximately four minutes a day or twenty-six minutes extra daylight per week! Note that it's best to watch the sunrise half an hour before the actual rising as the colours are at their best beforehand, and likewise plan to stay half an hour after sunset for the same effect. Leave behind your mobile, your iPod and consciously allow your senses to be absorbed by the details, the formation of the clouds, their changing hues, the deepening blue of the background, the air on your skin, the first or last shafts of light upon your eyelids. Celebrate what an amazing artist is our God to have set the natural order into such conjunction. Give voice to your praise; or if you enjoy singing, take a lead from the psalmist:

I will sing and make music with all my soul,
Awake, harp and lyre! I will awaken the dawn.
   (Ps. 108:1-2)

Re-capture your child-like wonder and give it voice. Creation is there to enthral. If you have children, plan a sunset walk together – I remember my father doing that with us and these were special family moments of sharing.

Beauty in the small detail

There's grandeur in a mountain panorama, and great beauty too in the small detail. An ascent of Ben Hope in the clutches of a huge winter freeze made me aware of the beautiful traceries that frost and wind form at low temperatures – the concrete summit trig point was transformed into an art nouveau style piece of sculpture. Make the effort to see new things in what seems commonplace at a cursory glance. Study the stamen of a flower; a moss-grown wood; the varieties of shells and pebbles that make up a beach. Think of times when you have been amazed by the beauty of something seen – a new-born foal; the tiny hands and finger-nails of your first-born; the faint mauve of apple blossom;

the laden dew on hedgerow cobwebs. If you take photos, why not search for details to capture.

Consider that God is interested in the small details of our lives and isn't just there for the crisis. Cultivate the attitude of a young child towards a father who is interested in and responsive to our efforts to relate. Thank God for all the details He has finely orchestrated and how these combine into a form of symphonic sublimity to create the big picture grandeur.

Check the attitude that is always pressing on, racing against the clock, which so often fails to notice these details.

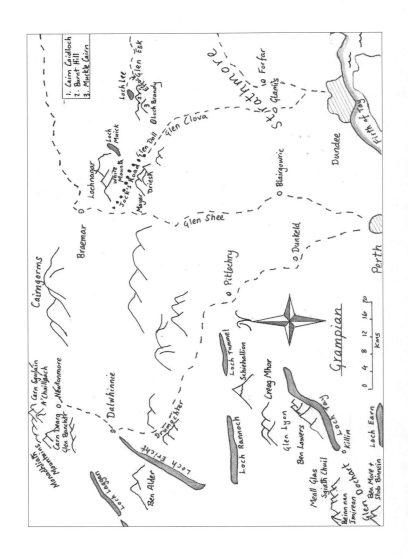

2

The Harsh Night

Driesh

A fresh start

AN extremely cold December night met my arrival at the bothy in the forests. This bothy was the first place of my own, an unpretentious home for the next year. I arrived in Glamis (see 'Grampian' map, p. 30) in 1976 still looking very much the student I had lately been: pale, with long hair and of fairly slight build. I had opted out of a legal career with the family firm in a deliberate quest for knowledge, to seek wisdom from a simple life working in forestry, close to nature. I felt driven to leave the unlovely place of Manchester where I had grown up, to escape the drink, the immature conjecture and youthful pretensions of college life that so recently had engulfed me.

'How long will mockers delight in mockery and fools hate knowledge?' (Prov. 1:22), echoes the objections that made me move on; a question presented to me caught up in youthful foolishness, rebelling against the values of those deemed successful. I sought knowledge beyond what I had gleaned from academia and when coming to books, I determined to fill in the perceived gaps in my education. I was desperate to flee from the arrogant swagger, the worldly pursuit and soulless hedonism of the society in which I had grown up, to follow my heart to source the inner poetry that I knew lay hidden deep within.

Just five miles north of Glamis, rose the Grampians; the nearest glen – Clova – an excellent example of a U-shaped valley, was clearly visible. At the upper reaches of Clova, the glen narrows and with its ever steepening slopes and much higher tops, takes on the name of Glen Doll. For much of that winter it was snow and ice bound, the sight of which kept me from pursuing the greater heights, being maybe a tad too cautious in hindsight. This was partly due to Bob, the saw-miller, who enjoyed spinning a yarn whenever possible to a naïve, young English lad new to the area. For someone who appeared to be just your standard labourer, Bob had a hidden side. He relished biographies of adventurers. Knowing the lure of the hills had brought me to Scotland, Bob spoke of heroic endeavours and misfortunes. His own telling of these stories tended to be based on the truth but with many embellishments. Recounted with such vivacity, and accompanied by a wicked wheeze of a laugh, the suggestion was that these were all just one big tease. But anyone who dared contest the accuracy would be summarily silenced by one of his impassioned salvos, 'It's true, I'm tellin' yae!' said with such a threatening look, that most desisted from refuting his claims.

Shattered dreams

Come mid-March, I was tired of being kept from the Grampians, a feeling exacerbated by weeks of back-breaking work stooping to set out saplings in the nursery. Heartened by a thaw, I set off one Friday night straight after work for Glen Doll; a bid for freedom after many long weeks feeling disillusioned by the reality of the forester/poet existence. I hadn't anticipated the exhaustion caused by labouring from 7.30 a.m. through to 5 p.m. with only a three-quarter hour lunch break. I had imagined evenings after work, pouring out my soul over pages of poetry in an idyll of creativity, never expecting to be so tired as to be mentally incapacitated.

My preconceived notions of the country labourer fed by Wordsworthian romanticism were quite contrary to the men I encountered. They had the same passions as those in the cities: obsessive about football, drinking to excess, womanising, always moaning about the unfairness of their pay and the unjust decisions of those above, always on the lookout to take things easy. These were major knocks in the pursuit of the noble ideal I strived for. I distanced myself from them to flee from so much sordid talk, the result of which unknown to me at the time, caused me to nurture a proud spirit. But all of this was about to be challenged.

Reality check

Hitching to Glen Clova, I relished the walk along the traffic-free road up the glen, enthralled by the corries coming into view above Glen Doll; mountain scenery I had longed to see close up since arriving in Scotland three months earlier. My frustrations had driven me to overnight in whatever shelter I might find in Glen Doll. Desperation and pride made me forfeit taking bed and breakfast at the Clova Hotel, opting instead for a roofless ruin a couple of miles further on.

There I was humbled at the feet of Driesh, the high peak looming over Glen Doll. Whilst not remote or of great altitude, the ordeal rose out of the primitive nature of what I had brought with me: T-shirt, shirt, knitted sweater, a donkey jacket and a big plastic bag without any insulation or breathable membrane, just literally a thin but durable plastic, like a deep rubble sack into which I climbed and lay for a long March night of sub-zero temperatures. My proud spirit was about to be broken.

A passing shadow

The hours of darkness in mid-March are many in Scotland. Twelve long hours, prolonging the ordeal of a terrible damp and then freezing night. I bedded down on a disarray of rotting timber boards with the bare modicum of a plastic survival bag to preserve life. The lasting impression I had was of staring up through the fallen roof on to a rocky, outlying spur of Driesh looking sardonically down upon this frail mortal. Driesh is derived from the Gaelic for a thorn bush or bramble – and prick me it certainly did! All night long, I shifted from oblivion to long protracted portions of time when death seemed a likely outcome as my body numbed with cold gave way to muted consciousness when awake. The stoic form of the ageless hills between me and the stars drew out an internal monologue resulting in acceptance of my lot, and discovery of peace. The monumental disappointments caused by my lack of perspective were now downsized by the real fear of dying and the appreciation for the simple, the necessary things that sustain life. Driesh appeared to laugh condescendingly; me a passing shadow across a landscape that in a man's span of years would remain quite changeless. The psalmist expresses such thoughts:

As for man, his days are like grass, he flourishes like a
    flower of the field;
The wind blows over it and it is gone, and its place
    remembers it no more. (Ps. 103:15-16)

Pivot point

I began to rediscover and appreciate all that I had sought
in coming to Scotland. The thrill of having my first home,
gratitude at moving on from the frivolity of student life,
to experience the world beyond the cushioned confines of
twentieth-century living. I saw the bothy in its true light,
a shelter from the raw elemental forces of the northlands
which was life-preserving, but also a refuge of comfort,
familiarity and peace. These things I had fully appreciated
only after the exposure of that harsh night. Subsequently,
the life I came to live shaped me (as opposed to the fruitless
task of me trying to shape the life the way I wanted and
expected it to be). This provided a training ground for me
to develop as a poet; an opportunity I never had when
studies and other pursuits distracted me. This pivotal point
of acceptance brought a sense of freedom and the wild
grandeur of my surroundings in contrast to my urban life
was a huge reward. The toil of labour was a small price.
Forestry provided a livelihood, developed me physically
and kept me from the office tasks I would have despised.
Whatever the dullness of some of the repetitive jobs
I had, these were compensated for by working in such
inspirational surroundings and I made it my intent to lift
up my eyes and take note. I learned not only to tolerate
my fellow labourers but to see the silver emerge from out
of the dross.

I came of age that long night beneath Driesh. Here was an encounter with something far greater, wiser and more lasting than myself, enabling me to begin to understand the sentiments expressed in this soul-seeking proverb:

If you ... turn your ear to wisdom and apply your heart to understanding ... and cry aloud for understanding, and if you look for it as for silver and search for it as for hidden treasure, then you will understand the fear of the Lord and find the knowledge of God.   (Prov. 2:1-5)

This northern outlying spur of Driesh, seen from the valley floor of Doll, is much more impressive than the rather tame rounded summit climbed later that year. Without this mid-March night-long encounter, I doubt Driesh would have featured among my most memorable of the Scottish hills – a peak that restored order in my universe.

MEDITATION

'The Harsh Night'

That freezing night spent in a roofless ruin in mid-March, restored equilibrium to a world that had become distorted through my own unhelpful pre-conceptions of the kind of life I expected to live. Instead of being at odds with all that fell far short of my anticipated ideals, my eyes had been opened to see the simple blessings all too easily taken for granted. I kept these as reminders when I began to see things out of kilter again.

Instead of wistfully dreaming that things would be different, consciously list all you can be thankful for that's so easily taken for granted. This goes a long way to finding contentment, as Paul reminds us in 1 Timothy 6:6-8:

But godliness with contentment is great gain. For we brought nothing into the world, and we can take nothing out of it. But if we have food and clothing, we will be content with that.

Things to be thankful for can include your family, your home, a shelter from the cold, food on the table even if it's only baked beans on toast. Continue the list and consider these are all blessings from God. If you find the exercise difficult, imagine an invading force had destroyed your home and car and you were on the run. What would become the essential needs that you would strive to get? This exercise is the reality for some in other lands and by the grace of God we're not caught up in these upheavals. Allow this thankfulness to redress the things that we have a big moan about (lack of a parking space, a development next to your house that will impact your environment). Allow this to make you reconsider how you might give to charity.

Consider a time of extreme hardship that had the effect of a refining process, helping you better come to terms with circumstances that previously you were at odds with. What were the issues that had so bothered you? Are these still issues? What helped you change perspective? Are you usually still maintaining that perspective?

As you work through this process, thank God afresh for such breakthroughs. Consciously try to keep these as reminders, checking the old patterns of thought and so deliberately 'be transformed by the renewing of your mind' (Rom. 12:2).

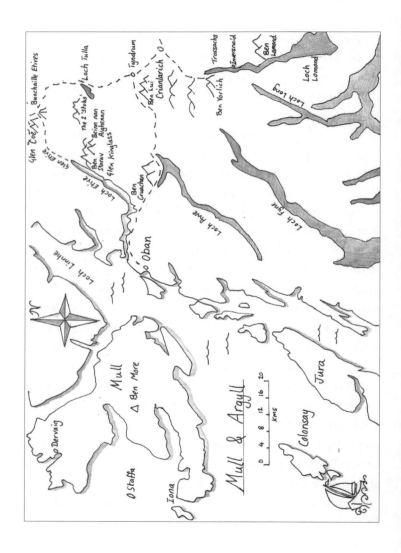

Mull & Argyll

38

3

In Father's Footsteps

Ben More, Mull

Like father like son

LOVE for the Scottish hills was born in me one summer's fortnight when our family rented a farm cottage near Dervaig on the Isle of Mull (see 'Mull and Argyll' map, p. 38). Aged eleven, I recall a magnificent holiday of sunbathing on beaches, making treks down single-track roads ribboned by yellow gorse and broom vivid against a backdrop of a serene sea beneath a near cloudless dome of sky. The tide created a rhythm that coaxed one to shift pace. This was the 1960s, an era of far fewer cars, a world where Mull seemed a far-distant place, a truly different world, a Hebridean island that enticed one across the straits.

Ben More rose tantalisingly into my father's sights, its airy heights seemed conjured out of a summer trance, rising ethereal above the Atlantic. It just beckoned to be climbed. We parked in a lay-by to the north of the hill and instead of crossing the road to start the ascent, my father turned towards the sea below.

'We'll go down to the water's edge and you can dip your toe in before climbing the peak.' I must have looked at him quizzically for he added, 'You'll have started from sea level and then can say you've climbed every foot of the hill.'

Ben More is the perfect starter Munro. The highest peak and the only Munro on the island, or on any other island other than Skye, it commands a view of much of Mull's sizeable bulk. Ben More enticed with a Robinson Crusoe like curiosity to climb to its summit and appreciate the island's topography of deep inlets and vast peninsulas.

I owe my love of the hills to my father who created in me an appreciation for the wide-open spaces, the sometime far-reaching views and the intense satisfaction of reaching the top. He instilled a passion for adventure. Formative memories were of my mother dropping him off early morning at the foot of some hill ridge draped in cloud and then much later, at the other end of the day, in a far distant place, of waiting for him to emerge from the seeping mist; in the eyes of his son, a returning hero. I secretly marvelled at his ability to find his way through cloud and storm, cover great distances over rugged and remote terrain, and yet make little of the feat.

Training

Then came the day when I was taken on a trip; a lesser trip, but a hill adventure nonetheless. A new bond between father and son grew out of the implicit trust I placed in my dad. What seemed complex to just a young lad, filled me with admiration for my dad as he used his skills to bring us through the hills, no matter how poor the visibility, and lead us safely back to the car by a round route. There were, however, moments when I had to be coaxed – times when I whinged a good deal. Once in the Pennines unable to go any further, I sheltered in a barn with my two older sisters. They, only too aware of the dangers of hypothermia, kept a rather reluctant younger brother warm by having me play energetic games, whilst my father walked six miles to fetch the car.

'Train a child in the way he should go, and when he is old he will not turn from it' – runs an ancient proverb (Prov. 22:6) and that rang true for me. The proverb applies to many things parents can pass down. The hillwalking legacy, and all that goes with it was part of my training: orienteering, purposeful attitude, perseverance, appreciation of the wilds, a fascination for topography. More significant was finding peace within myself, in tune with nature and experiencing the dawn of a spiritual awakening. And what I valued when out in the hills with another person was being able to truly relate, the ability to understand that comes from passing an entire day together with few distractions. Absent, or retiring fathers, deprive their children of so much. I am grateful for my father's persistence in enticing a sometime reluctant lad from lesser pursuits to benefit from his encouragement. He would keep me going rather than give in to my complaints about being too cold, or foot-sore or it being too steep and too far. The ability to pace myself for the entire walk and to refrain from resting for too long and so avoid the consequences of stiffening up was knowledge passed down. He made me aware of our frailty in the face of adverse winter weather, of our brief passing through the age-old hills, a fleeting shadow in the eternal scheme of things. Awakened to the sense of affinity we have with this created order, he set my soul on the quest to seek spiritual enlightenment.

Ben More rises steadily, not exasperatingly steep and unrelentingly like its mainland namesake near Crianlarich. It rewards without gargantuan effort. The isle of Staffa rises bravely out at sea, where some days earlier, we had marvelled at the cathedral-like nave of Fingal's Cave; and Iona lay beyond the tip of the extensive peninsula, about which the poet Kenneth Steven wrote:

> *Is this place really nearer to God?*
> *Is the wall thin between our whispers*
> *And His listening? I only know*
> *The world grows less and less*
> *… I am not sure whether there is no time here*
> *Or more time, whether the light is stronger*
> *Or just easier to see. That is why*
> *I keep returning, thirsty to this place*
> *That is older than my understanding,*
> *Younger than my broken spirit.*   *Iona*[1]

Being there on top of Ben More I did feel closer to God; the dividing wall between us did seem thinner.

Gaining such a good first-time hill experience is helpful in establishing a love for hillwalking. Some are put off by being wet and chilled to the bone, or from being led by someone with exasperatingly poor navigational skills, leading to backtracking, or being forced too hard and too far. Such victims are difficult to entice back into the hills. This can be applied to leading others in life, such as parents

---

1. *Iona.* From collection entitled 'Iona' (Edinburgh: Saint Andrew Press, 2000), p. 18.

and their children, where the Bible warns fathers not to exasperate their offspring. I am indebted to my father for presenting a hill challenge that was possible and for sharing his skill and knowledge. He journeyed with me, the novice, passing on the resources to succeed and the eye to marvel.

MEDITATION

'In Father's Footsteps'

Thanks to the example of my father and through his encouragement, I began a lifelong love for the hills. Think of someone who helped cultivate a healthy interest/passion in you. Think of the Christian who was especially instrumental in helping you find faith, or the one who has helped to be a pointer along the way. How did they go about achieving that? What positive encouragements did you get from that person? Give thanks for their interest in helping shape you to become what you are today, aware too that God brought that person into your life.

Is there a legacy here that you can pass on to another person? How did they go about helping you? What attitude of theirs could you emulate in helping another? This might not be with the same interest, but is there an interest in another you can help develop and encourage? Consider what first step you can practically take to encourage that person.

Consider how Paul encouraged the young Timothy in 2 Timothy 1:3-7:

'I thank God … as night and day I constantly remember you in my prayers' (v. 3). How good it is to know that another person takes such an interest in us that they pray daily, giving thanks for who we are. Who comes to mind that we can commit to praying for daily?

'Recalling your tears, I long to see you, so that I may be filled with joy' (v. 4). Can we be more expressive in telling another person that they are valued, but with language appropriate to our culture that won't give concern?

'I have been reminded of your sincere faith, which first lived in your grandmother Lois and in your mother Eunice and, I am persuaded, now lives in you also' (v. 5). Paul calls to mind the faith of Timothy's family members, which like a legacy has become evident in his life. As he is keen to commend Timothy for a faith that shines in the ones he loves and respects, is there someone that could provide an aspirational model to the one you seek to encourage?

'For this reason I remind you to fan into flame the gift of God, which is in you through the laying on of my hands' (v. 6). What gentle encouragement can we convey for them to exercise a God-given gift or ability?

'For God did not give us a spirit of timidity, but a spirit of power, of love and of self-discipline' (v. 7). Youth and inexperience can lack confidence or conviction to step up to the mark. Sometimes encouragement can be a challenge to trust God for the work He is doing in them and for the gift He has given to be exercised for the benefit of others. What gifts do you perceive to be latent in the one you could encourage? Your word could give the direction and the confidence that perhaps they have been waiting for before they feel it's right to move forward.

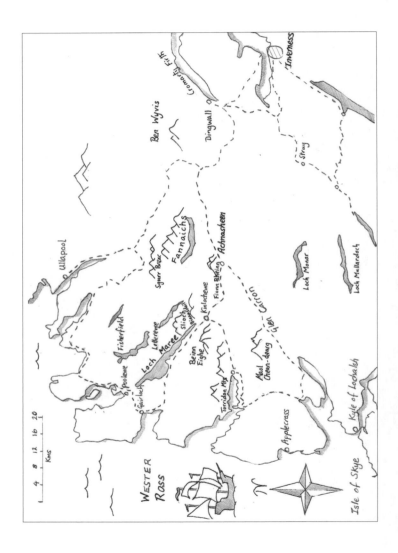

4

Despite the Odds

Fionn Bheinn and the Fannaichs

PULLING off the road at Achnasheen (see 'Wester Ross' map, p. 46) everywhere was white, and more storm clouds were blowing in. I sat in the warm car feeling sleepy after the journey, reluctant to move as skies darkened. Then it snowed heavily, sticking fast. Years ago I would have thrown in the towel there and then and although I still had concerns for my own preservation, I wasn't so quick to give up on the idea of walking, especially after driving several hours to arrive there having negotiated a day off work. I decided to just set out and see how conditions really were underfoot.

So I followed the Allt Achadh na Sine – the burn running between steep-sided braes – making the only distinguishable feature in this winter land. The snow still fell fast. I intended to be wise and turn around if the snow cover became too deep and considered this initial part more a stretch of the legs after being cooped up in a car for hours. But the snow cover, although solid white for sure, wasn't so deep and it wasn't that cold either. So I climbed on, setting my feet towards the unseen summit of Fionn Bheinn, a Munro just over the minimum height, relatively close to the road and not in the least technical. In other words an uninspiring hill and for anyone who knows the Munros, they might question my choice in including it – so low is the expectation it arouses. Even the meaning of its name – 'the pale-coloured hill' – doesn't really inspire!

When stars and angels shout for joy

After half an hour's ascent, it began to brighten and within the space of a few steps I left the choking freezing fog and snow to emerge into brilliant sunshine in a ringing blue sky! There at my feet wallowed a sea of cloud choking the strath below. What a transformation – who would have thought it! Considerably heartened, I pushed on, richly rewarded by a little stubbornness more positively termed perseverance. There was no telling where the path lay as I arrived at a gentle shelving basin, but the day was clear and the contours obvious leading up to the summit massif. These were even better conditions than a normal day as the boggy ground was frozen. I passed through a sunken way amidst irregular raised stacks of what must have been peat hags under the snow.

With it being late November when the hills had been clear a few days earlier, the snow had little depth. This greatly enhanced progress up the next section of steepening slopes until I reached a good ridge where the gradient was gentle and the sides fell away unthreateningly to the west and more abruptly to the east. The way broadened again until I came to Fionn Beinn with its corrie-like northern aspect facing the superb arc of the Fannaich Hills. Although I had climbed all the Fannaichs by then, I had never seen them in one group. The view took my breath away on this still summit; an awesome winter land of bold peaks rising steeply from beyond a seven-mile long loch, bathed in sunlight, resplendent, like a newly created earth, pure under its wraps of crystalline beauty. I sat down against the cairn overwhelmed by the splendour and majesty before me, privileged to have this glimpse after so unpromising a start, feeling dumbstruck and small. The words of the Lord to Job came to mind:

'*Where were you when I laid the earth's foundation?*
Tell me, if you understand.
Who marked off its dimensions?
Surely you know!
Who stretched a measuring line across it?
On what were its footings set,
Or who laid the cornerstone –
While the morning stars sang together
And all the angels shouted for joy? (Job 38:4-7)

I love that concept of stars and angels singing for joy over the marvels of God's handiwork. I identified Sgurr Breac at the western end of the Fannaichs bringing to mind a December climb in bitterly cold weather with a heavily frosted crust of snow on the peak. The wind had been so penetrating that day, feeling like a hole boring through my forehead creating that pain similar to eating ice cream, but with a threatening constancy. I had arrived on the summit dome in a sweat after climbing hard in Arctic conditions, and stopping for a minute, the sweat congealed to a clammy cold. I soon felt frozen to the core. I wanted to rest, just to succumb to the great sleepiness engulfing me. The light was frail and uncertain despite the whiteness of the summit. The pale tatters of cloud sweeping past made the light, even life itself, uncertain, transient, inducing this desire to rest. I liked the idea of scooping out a snow hole to shelter from this fiercely driven cold, to tumble into a world white upon white with the weary moan of the wind blowing above. I had stood upon this frail brink before, this edge of existence filled with the fanciful desire to push on to eternity's shore and leave the desperate world of toil behind. It made me conscious of our finite nature and the longing for the permanence of being with the Lord.

> Before the mountains were born or you brought forth
>   the earth and the world,
> From everlasting to everlasting you are God.
> You turn men back to dust saying 'Return to dust,
>   O sons of men.'
> For a thousand years in your sight are like a day that
>   has just gone by,
> Or like a watch in the night.
> You sweep men away in the sleep of death;
> They are like the new grass of the morning –
> Though in the morning it springs up new, by evening it
>   is dry and withered.   (Ps. 90:2-6)

Value your days

Brought to the brink, I willed to live, but not as before, rather desiring to have eternity bearing down on the present, shaping my days that none would be ill-spent. This brought to mind a verse from the same Psalm:

*Teach us to number our days aright, that we may gain
a heart of wisdom.* (Ps. 90:12)

The wind blew away the staleness from life, awakening me
to the need to avoid chasing too many ends, being driven by
demands, and to make choices that were noble and deliberate.
Determined to be genuine with God and to what was
authentic about myself, I wanted to be true to the vocation
and gifting that God had engraved on my personality.

How different it now was on Fionn Bheinn! This day was
a day of celebration, of surprise, as great in contrast as when
stepping from the frozen fog on to radiant ground. On the
descent down to the Allt Achadh na Sine, I stopped as the winter
shadows sprawled their huge coldness over the land, and took
some minutes just to lie in the snow looking at the blue sky and
back to Fionn Bheinn. In the light of the low sun, my solitary
trail through the snow made a line slightly brighter, tracing the
steady way up to that vantage point above Loch Fannich and
to the hills rising majestically beyond. A single trail expressing a
deliberation to overcome the apathy, a concerted effort to resist
the flabby surrender to compromise. I had communed once
more with my Maker and it had delivered a time of intense joy.

Some things in life can simply be not that appealing, or
perhaps don't promise much. Reluctance and apathy need
to be overcome by just goading yourself to give it a go,
to try things out and develop a hopeful, open attitude to
what appears to be very ordinary and unpromising. Circumstances may seem to conspire from going forward, but with
a little perseverance mixed with caution and an attitude of
optimism, this can help us to overcome, resulting in the
sheer surprise of an outstanding experience.

An example to bear this out would be the Israelites approaching the city of Jericho, high-walled and heavily defended, which was overwhelmed through faith and implicit trust in following the directions of the Lord; or the unpromising start on the day of Pentecost when some in the crowd made fun of the disciples who were enabled to speak in other languages by the ridicule, '"They have had too much wine"' (Acts 2:13).

Let us not presume that inauspicious beginnings cannot lead to amazing results with our God.

MEDITATION

'Despite the Odds'

The prospect of climbing the unspectacular hill of Fionn Bheinn didn't particularly excite me and in wintry conditions too, was it wise? But the surprise of breaking through the cloud cover, of leaving wintry storm and gloom for the hills bathed in sunlight caused me to marvel and to wonder. Contemplate a view that lifts your spirits – spend some unhurried time marvelling at the variety and the colours in the landscape and let it prompt the praise of 'one-liners', acknowledging the works of God as Creator.

But God made the earth by his power;
He founded the world by his wisdom
And stretched out the heavens by his understanding.
When he thunders, the waters in the heavens roar;
He makes clouds rise from the ends of the earth.
He sends lightning with the rain
And brings out the wind from his storehouses.
    (Jer. 10:12-13)

Such monumental works of creation and the mystery of the weather and our slight tenure on earth felt in the grip of cold and storm, can make us re-evaluate our lives and to live intentionally, not driven all the time by circumstance. Examine what drives you daily. Are these things part of your chosen agenda? What counts in the eternal scheme of things? If necessary, re-evaluate your priorities and allow these to be a compass bearing by which to pursue noble aims and goals.

Think of an event (it doesn't have to be a hill walk) that really didn't promise very much but in the end turned out to be quite a surprise and a blessing. It's all too easy to not bother with something that doesn't promise much at the outset. To have an open mind, to make an effort can lead to surprise. Pray that this attitude could be cultivated in you more.

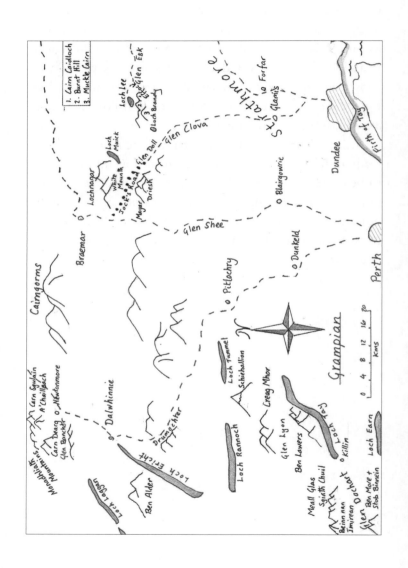

54

5

Not Alone

Lochnagar

'IT'S one heck of a hill! Claimed many a life!' was how Bob, the saw-miller, first drew my attention to Lochnagar (see 'Grampian' map, p. 54). 'It's quite a height, yae ken, and the temperatures can fall well below zero, especially wi' all the wind chill.' There is something magical about this hill, even in the very name, the only Munro named after its loch that's inspired a poem by no less than Byron.

This likeable rogue further coaxed me, 'Nae for the faint-hearted, yae ken – only fir those wi' a thirst fir a great feat!' Bob was very much the armchair adventurer, quite excelling at transforming a simple tale of a day out in the hills into the stuff of legend. Without equal at spinning a yarn, he conjured epic exploits, treading upon the very brink between here and eternity.

Rising significantly above its wild, expansive mountain plateau, it's the height and character of Lochnagar that inspires. Without doubt it's the grand prize in this area of the Grampians. I had first seen this peak in early May when walking from Glen Esk to Glen Clova – one of my first forays of my year in Glamis. That first winter I had been constantly champing at the bit looking north across the Vale of Strathmore to the Highlands, my hopes raised of a first sortie into real hills each weekend. More than once I let excitement grow as snows thawed only for my plans to be dashed a day or two later by a fresh fall of snow.

I had set off straight after work, taking a lift with Bob as far as Forfar and then hitching to Brechin and on to Edzell to the start of the lovely Glen Esk. The birch was fresh in leaf, and a lovely sunny and still evening so enthralled that the fatigue of the working week just evaporated. The lure of the open road and a glen quite unknown to me, stretching a good twenty kilometres to the road end just short of Loch Lee urged me on. A farmer took me a good distance along the glen, otherwise I would have been walking literally half the night to reach the top. At dusk, I struck southwest up Glen Effock, climbing out of the dampness of the river valley, up the flank of Cairn Caidloch and Burnt Hill. Before reaching the ridge, I laid out my survival bag among a thick growth of heather and put on every item of clothing from my small backpack. Pulling a woolly hat over my ears, I bedded down on to a comfortable mattress of heather. The bleat of the sheep at first seemed quaint, but before long reminded me that I was a stranger to this environment, especially as the night chill made sleeping fretful at best. The lemon glow of cottage lights down in Glen Esk made me long for shelter to escape the alien sensation of the yawning depths of the starry spread of the universe above my head. The night seemed interminable and late on, the ground was so frosted that my beard froze to the collar of my jacket, fastened by the moisture of my breath.

Created for a purpose

First light revealed a sky that transformed from an inky dark to a lovely egg-shell blue without a cloud overhead. Regaining feeling to each numbed limb was a painful experience, each stride a slow liberation of every muscle fibre from aching torpor. I began to feel energised, full of anticipation of the view from the summit. A blue hare in the heather shot out from beneath my feet with the remnants of his winter coat showing white. Then the summit was reached, all 647 m of it. Far from grand and of no consequence to a Munro-bagger but it was a well-positioned summit. Loch Lee lay still, inert, unwakened by the kiss of dawn. But morning light streamed upon this hill top; its horizontal rays giving a warm glow, suffusing life into the frosty ridges, its rich amber depicting every rock and cliff and steep brae with vivid distinction. High up, a jet left a noiseless trail of vapour across the perfectly clear sky. I imagined the plane's occupants fast asleep, perhaps bound for Canada or the States. And if anyone should have looked down on this section of the Grampians, it wouldn't have seemed spectacular. But for me, having endured a frosty night in the open and now free from the numbing pain, I felt electrifyingly alive, at one with my environment. I was alone, the only witness to the pristine beauty of a dawn in the hills. All that morning I had a heroic sense of being invincible, every limb felt so vibrant that I thought myself capable of any feat. At that epochal moment, youth had matured into manhood, and all things seemed possible. Every bounding stride was a celebration of energy bringing the knowledge that I had been 'fearfully and wonderfully made' (Psalm 139:14). The undulating way over to Loch Brandy by way of Muckle Cairn was a breeze completed without tiring.

This walk was a defining moment. Knowing I had been created for a purpose, that my soul, sensitive to the created order around me, held communion with the One who had made everything around, including me. At that time I didn't go to church, I didn't read the Bible, or any other sacred texts and yet instinctively I knew I was not alone, that I wasn't created by some random chance, but that God had made a wonderfully complex and finely balanced universe and an earth where life was possible and had placed me there, made in His image and responsive to all He had made. A Creator who desired to make Himself known. This is wisdom, imparted and divinely made known. This is what I lived for, the desire that led me back time and again to learn, to be shaped, to mature and grow in knowledge and wisdom of the Lord.

> *Blessed is the man who finds wisdom, the man who gains*
>   *understanding,*
> *For she is more profitable than silver and yields better*
>   *returns than gold …*
> *Her ways are pleasant ways, and all her paths are peace.*
> *She is a tree of life to all who embrace her; those who lay*
>   *hold of her will be blessed.*   (Prov. 3:13-14, 17-18)

Along this way from Esk to Clova, I had my first sighting of Lochnagar, eighteen kilometres away into the Grampian hinterland, rising stark, asserting its prominence above the flow of rounded hills. Such a summit makes a lasting impression, exerting a growing fascination and restlessness that can't be dispelled until one climbs it.

This ascent of Lochnagar from Glen Doll was not the typical approach, the start usually being made from Balmoral. But this would have made for a long car journey from Glamis. Not only is it longer, but it entails more height due to the additional climb out of the deep trough of Loch Muick over the pass for the return to Glen Doll.

My route from Glen Doll north towards Braemar, was along 'Jock's Road' where Bob told me about five experienced hillwalkers who lost their lives up on the plateau in a wind chill of −25°. The winter of 1959 was so severe that it took four months before their bodies could be retrieved. Bob teased of how so many people despairing of reaching their journey's end, had turned back before mid-way – so went the predictable yarn that prompted nods and 'ayes' from the other foresters, either out of ignorance, or for the fun of goading a young English lad in awe of the Scottish hills. My respect for Lochnagar was raised further by my father having to cut his losses when snow fell thick and fast on a past foray.

New ways

If I hadn't been so determined and had I not learned my hill-craft from my father, these comments might have deterred me from a solo exploit of climbing Lochnagar from Glen Doll. It's true of life: think of doing something quite new and you can guarantee a volley of well-meant advice and warnings of dangers that easily erode what little confidence we had at the outset. It takes some knowledge and calculation, mixed with gritty determination, to attempt something out of the ordinary and prove our detractors wrong. Knowledge gleaned from the hills has made me steadfast in pursuing goals in life that have appeared audacious and risky to others.

I had hitched a lift up Glen Clova the night before and walked the final three miles to the youth hostel at Glen Doll. Back in the mid-seventies, the hostel warden was a white-haired, leonine man who seemed the epitome of one living content and at peace in the deep fastness of the hills. I had expected my fellow foresters to be like this man, one who had great dignity. But I didn't know the warden's character; just that his appearance complied with my preconceived conceptions of how man should be content in a rural environment, exhibiting a noble quality. But I had come to appreciate the flip sides to likeable rogues like Bob, who although not conforming to what I had hoped to find, did provide colour and humour to a life without which things would be much more mundane. It required looking beyond the brash exterior to see the inner humanity. This second take on people exposed my own sense of superiority, and led me to admire their knowledge of the forest and bird life, fencing and tree felling skills and all manner of wisdom. Theirs was and is an earthly wisdom that lends dignity to, and relationship with, the environment around.

The following morning the weather was fair and Jock's Road was not the arduous toil Bob would have me believe, but made for a pleasant start along a track with the peaks of Mayar and Driesh across the forested glen to the south providing a reference to mark the quick progress. On reaching the rim of the corrie, the open expanse of the Grampian tops unfolded giving the sense of ascending towards the big prize. Ahead rose the massif of the White Mounth from which thirteen Munros rise from a high plateau – a region where several Munros can be reached without difficulty in a day. What far-reaching views there were of other regions, quite unknown to me as without car and only a scant knowledge of Scotland's geography, I had a very patchy idea of the progressive development of the landscape beyond the near horizon. The distant suggestion of the Cairngorms came on to my radar that day, their unknown topography alluring me, heightening expectations and providing grand possibilities.

Views down on to Deeside's pine forests, the steep descent to Loch Muick past impressive waterfalls, the passage around the head of the loch followed by the unrelenting ascent to complete the traverse back to Glen Doll made it a grand day's walk, all adding significantly to the satisfaction of climbing Lochnagar. The path down to Glen Doll is a delight as it zig-zags into the spring green of the larch, to a footbridge over a small rocky gorge – making a charming place distinct from the sprawling desolations of the vast rolling uplands. Trees, like people, which grow in challenging environments shaped by decades of storms and frost, stand out from the crowd.

It's the account of this that inspired my head forester to tackle the same route himself and made for another fine outing in his company. Although a very fit man, he complained of his muscles seizing up on the interminable ascent up from Loch Muick at the day's end. But he succeeded and this made it more the epic.

MEDITATION

'Not Alone'

Walking and overnighting on the open hillside in just a survival bag in the locality of Lochnagar was a defining moment in recognising God. Then followed a rare day when hillwalking seemed effortless (it was many years ago!) and

I felt unstoppable, so full of vitality that it was positively overflowing.

Had I been a Christian at that point, I would have declared:

> *The sovereign Lord is my strength;*
> *He makes my feet like the feet of a deer,*
> *He enables me to go on the heights.* (Hab. 3:19)

In retrospect though I would maintain that the Lord gives strength, even to those who don't seek or acknowledge Him. Consider how the Lord enables you to rise and to succeed. Acknowledge Him in each aspect that comes to mind.

As a non-professing Christian at the time, I was made very conscious of being 'fearfully and wonderfully made', an awareness of the works of the Creator being tremendous and that life was to be spent in the pursuit of wisdom, of knowing God.

Consider a formative time when you grew conscious of God, when His presence was first perceived. It can be as simple and yet as profound as a wee lad I know telling his dad at the breakfast table of seeing a star through the new Velux installed in his bedroom. Full of wonder, he had found it difficult to close his eyes. This might not be a conversion moment, but one of those early times when God was seeking you out, getting your attention, touching your spirit.

Relive that moment, recapture those awakening thoughts and feelings. Give thanks to God for the evidences of His reality. Think how you might make others aware of such wonder.

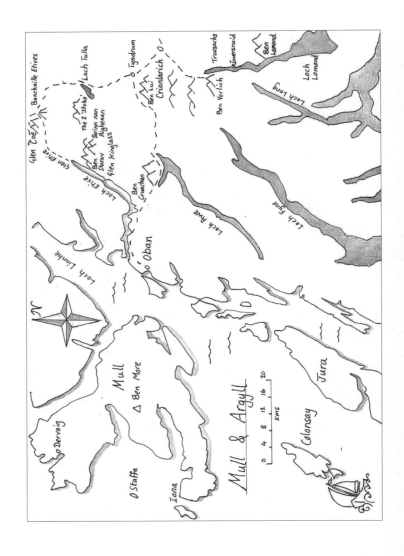

Mull & Argyll

64

6

Being Approved

Ben Lui

The best laid plans

THE twin peaks of Ben Lui (see 'Mull and Argyll' map, p. 64), like two pointed extremities rising either side of a saddle, are only briefly glimpsed from the A82 when travelling north to Tyndrum. It's a shy hill but once seen, continues to entice. Ben Lui was to be the final peak of the first day of an ambitious longer trek, a venture my father offered to support by driving ahead to a suitable rendezvous. The plan was that he would walk out to meet me on the agreed route and we would walk back together to the car where we would camp, avoiding the need to carry a tent or having to resort to sleeping in a survival bag. On the off chance we failed to meet, two points were plotted on the map between which the car would be parked where we would coincide at the end of the day.

This upland version of the West Highland Way was to be a great opportunity to appreciate and to become intimate with an extensive corridor of scenery way up into the heart of the Highlands. We planned the route between us, poring over maps, measuring horizontal distances and vertical ascent and descent and in the process forming a mental image of the landscape, noting the impassable places of corries and lochs, wary of the flatness of bogs. The relationship between walker and surroundings grows as you look from the great vantage point of the heights back along the way you've made on the laborious ascent. Next you preview the onward section, sizing up the terrain, tracing the obvious route, noting the features of boulders, heather, crag and stream in case the mist descends and then this snapshot can guide together with map and compass. Then there's the review as you take your final glance back on all the miles trodden, the heights scaled, the ridges traversed, the descent down the cleft in the corrie, images that replay all evening until they fade as the body melts into sleep at the end of a wholly memorable day. The mood of having walked far and climbed several peaks isn't triumphalistic – more the rich fulfilment of knowing the character and spirit of an area intimately – an intimacy that fades in time but enables one to maintain a great fondness of place redolent with particular memories.

Being dropped at the northern end of Loch Lomond created a twenty-six kilometre long hike north with only four kilometres on any kind of path with the remainder over wild ground. The route took in Ben Vorlich and three more eminent ridges to traverse with valley drops between, involving a total climb of 1,860 metres before arriving at the final destination of the Tyndrum–Oban road. The trouble was my father overestimated my ability and truth be told, the greater enthusiasm for this epic walk was more his. Only years later, frustrated by the limitations of walking round trips, and with much improved stamina, did I come to highly value a willing backup driver to facilitate a walk in one direction.

By the time I made it over the third ridge and then dropped a further thousand feet, my strength was quite spent. It was tough just to make the col west of Ben Lui, let alone reach the summits, from where I could look down to the finish: the Oban–Tyndrum road. The evening was well advanced and although downhill all the way, progress was hampered by what were then new coniferous plantations with high deer fences to scale and deep drainage ditches to scamper over or to detour around.

Having ascended Ben Lui and continued down into the glen to the south, my father had long since returned to the car for the night. I eventually came upon him bedding down in the deepening dusk, making it well gone 11 p.m. in June. He was visibly relieved to see me, one of only two times when he showed any trace of relief ending a keenly felt anxiety. The other time was again my arriving late, this time a week overdue for a holiday together on Corfu; the cause of delay being the outbreak of the Iraq/Iran war in September 1980 keeping me in Baghdad.

He had been scouring his eyes over the braes of Ben Lui for most of the evening, hoping to catch sight of a solitary hiker. I recall him talking very jovially as we camped down side by side in the car, telling me he had decided to wait until morning before alerting the mountain rescue.

The next day brought rain which together with feeling very stiff and drained from the previous day's ordeal, consumed any eagerness for another long trek north. I groan inwardly now at my passing up of this stellar opportunity of being supported to do such a route. Of course the best remedy for stiffness is more exercise to loosen the muscles, something I didn't appreciate then.

Connection

In reality though I don't regret calling off the epic journey owing to the very special time I had with my father. We ended up based at my bothy for the remainder of the fortnight, making daily sorties by car to climb several peaks together. My father eulogised about my woodsman's existence, very much in sympathy with the choice I had made not to join the family law firm. His approval meant much, especially in view of my recent struggles in coming to terms with the realities. Being together for days on end, with no one else, no television or other distractions brought a transparency we hadn't had before or were to fully experience quite the same way again. It's easy to never fully connect and be disarmingly honest with another person. Wearied of the legal profession, my father envied my choice of a simple life, encouraging me to be content with little and to enjoy to the full being at one with the natural environment. Too late for him to turn back the clock so in a sense he lived vicariously through what I had chosen; a dream he cherished more as his years advanced. His counsel, refined from decades in the professional workplace, reminded me of the following precept:

Better one handful with tranquillity than two handfuls with toil and chasing after the wind. (Eccles. 4:6)

The tranquillity of a wee place in the country was indeed tremendous and he opened up, sharing aspirations and regrets and yet still maintaining a fatherly encouragement to be true to myself, to pursue things of value and not to chase empty riches or the vanity of prestige.

Upon my request, he brought a selection of classical music after I found my rock collection discordant and out of sync with the peace that was increasingly mine. My love for classical music was born in those days although I had imbibed their melodies from hearing them played in the family home. He introduced me to a broad spectrum, ranging from Mozart to Sibelius, setting up points of reference leading to ecstatic discoveries over the coming months. After a couple of extravagant shopping trips to Dundee, I had a basic classical collection. He delighted to see a son show a sensitivity to the natural world, who followed in his footsteps of scaling mountains, who was at ease in solitude and found perfect expression of the inner tranquillity through this new-found love. He declared that music had never before sounded so eloquent and grand than when heard in that undisturbed environment. The delight evident in this togetherness steadied and strengthened my hand and established me in knowing myself better and understanding more of what I really sought in life.

I reflected upon all of this twenty years later when I finally joined my father's footsteps to the fine summit of Ben Lui. His climbing days, indeed his very life, had been abruptly cut off by a brain haemorrhage before reaching retirement, dashing the dream of moving to the hills of northern England. The refrain to keep true to what's essential and genuine about yourself, has remained a compass bearing along life's way to this day, leading me purposefully when making choices, steadying me through the various turbulent challenges of adapting to different cultures yet not losing the very essence of who I am and what makes me authentically myself. A father's word at the outset of adulthood has encouraged amidst doubts thrown up by the inevitable detractors who devalue the higher way taken. Such affirmation has at critical times given me the confidence to forge ahead when alone in one's convictions. After losing my father, I later gained a Father when I recognised God was seeking me, a lost wayfarer. Coming to know God as Father has been so significant, for I am no longer alone and have a means to communicate with and hear from a heavenly Father through His word and by His Spirit giving emphasis to that word. So my heavenly Father says to me:

Get wisdom …
Esteem her, and she will exalt you;
Embrace her, and she will honour you.
She will set a garland of grace on your head
And present you with a crown of splendour.
(Prov. 4:5, 8-9)

MEDITATION

'Being Approved'

Sometimes grand plans don't work out as hoped. The multiple-day hill expedition failed, but created a special opportunity to connect with my father which wouldn't have happened to such a degree had our plans succeeded.

Think of a time when good resulted from something that initially seemed disappointing. What was it that helped that connection? If another was involved, what did you most appreciate about their approach to relating? Consider how you could likewise relate to someone and be intentional in bringing that about, asking the Lord to bless those efforts.

Simon Peter was reluctant to let down his nets in broad daylight when you would least expect to catch fish and in front of his townsfolk and fellow fishermen. He protested to Jesus, 'Master, we've worked hard all night and haven't caught anything. But because you say so, I will let down the nets' (Luke 5:5). But because he determined to trust Jesus, even against his attitude of knowing better, he and the other fishermen were 'astonished' by such a large catch that their nets began to break and their boats began to sink under the weight. For Peter it was his huge pivotal point in acknowledging Jesus as Lord. What had been a fruitless night of fishing had been used by Jesus to reveal to Peter that He was Lord over creation.

How might you listen to God the Father, or Jesus, in the same way as Peter?

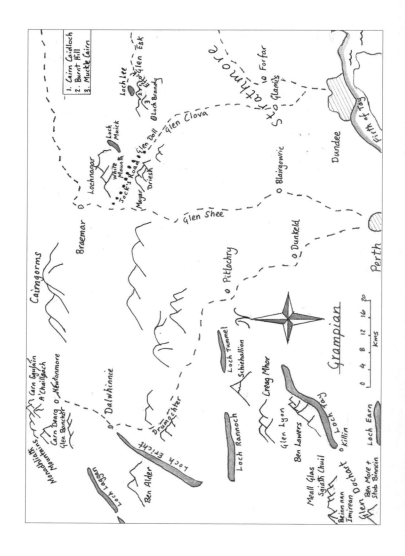

7

Seeking Direction

Ben Lawers

AN interval of four years lapsed from the last of the Grampian hills climbed during my time as a forester until the next ascent. This interval saw many changes. I had brought my time in Scotland to a close, taking up the invitation to teach English in Italy and join my sister there. I ended up as contracts manager for four years with an Italian engineering company, first working in Libya and then latterly in Iraq, via a number of other Arab states. After my father died suddenly, I worked out my notice so I could return home and help my mother get her life back on track. A holiday in Scotland soon followed, bringing with it a sense of homecoming to the hills and glens and the Scottish friends that I had so often missed when cooped up in air-conditioned offices and hotel bedrooms to escape the infernal heat of Arab cities in the summer.

We stayed in Dunblane with friends, a location providing me with a day's excursion to see my former workmates at Glamis, visit my bothy and walk the well-familiar haunts on the castle estate. Great as it was to catch up with good friends, I missed having a home in the forests, the loss of a deep tranquillity, my place of refuge and great learning. One particularly sunny day as my mother and I were picnicking on the shores of Loch Earn, the call of the hills summoned. I determined to do the round of five Munro summits along the Ben Lawers range (see 'Grampian' map, p. 72), including the peak itself – Perthshire's highest and just short of 4,000 feet – an ambitious jaunt in view of the long lethargy induced by boiling Baghdad.

The following day was dry but overcast with a freshness in the air – ideal for hillwalking. Looking down the twenty-one kilometre length of Loch Tay and to the immense array of peaks and ridges to the north, all quite unknown to me, made it especially memorable. Once the main ridge was reached, the group of five made an exhilarating circuit, the next peak just enticing me on. The relative and surprising ease of the walk gave me pause for lengthy rests on each summit and a chance to reflect over recent events.

Loss

My father's death was a great loss – a soulmate unexpectedly taken and without substitute. His death hit with agonising rawness and regret of not having spent more time with him latterly.

This return to hillwalking after four years scorching in the desert heat playing the commercial executive, connected me with what my father loved and therefore brought him much to mind. Taken from this life before his time, there appeared unfinished business in the hills for me to do on his behalf. It made me recall the extraordinary fortnight we spent together when communication barriers were removed.

With it came encouragement to opt for a simpler life, to be in harmony with the world around and take hold of what was true and enduring that would provide rest for the soul. The sudden passing of my mentor brought a renewed desire to acquire wisdom, to gain convictions from which to make right choices. I had been used to talking things through with a man who placed a different value on things. I had already been challenged by a well-meaning friend that it wasn't right, or to be expected, to turn from my established place in the business world of the Middle East to look after my mother. But I held fast, believing this to be a right and compassionate response at that particular time.

Going to the hills that day helped with the sorting of priorities, putting issues and personal concerns in the context of bigger realities and allowed me to grapple with difficulties without distractions. I could sense my own father's encouragement through the urge of this proverb to be true in my pursuit of spiritual knowledge.

Get wisdom, get understanding;
Do not forget my words or swerve from them.
Do not forsake wisdom, and she will protect you;
Love her, and she will watch over you. (Prov. 4:5-6)

There are various possible meanings to the name Ben Lawers – 'claw, hoof, big sound'. I like all three because some profound sense was knocked into me that day. The vast panoramas helped me gain fresh perspective, with time out from all the commercial cheating and political chicanery of the business world and the taut political tensions of living in the Middle East. It had been hard to achieve clarity of mind to process events from the shreds of time that such a life throws up. A proverb that likens delving into the deeper desires of what to do with one's life as to drawing waters from a well, speaks of something that is purposeful, requiring intention and isn't simply available at the turning on of a tap.

The purposes of a man's heart are deep waters
But a man of understanding draws them out.
(Prov. 20:5)

Peace

Time to reflect was invariably frustrated by the interruptions and distractions of the ceaseless restlessness and commerce about me in the Middle East. Up there on the ridge was a place beyond demands. The exercise had made me feel energetic and clear-headed, giving a strong sense of youthful courage, a resurgence of convictions held before my days of international commerce, convictions I had never really let go of, but rather had put to one side.

My Italian boss hadn't accepted my resignation. Instead he remarked, 'Go and have a long holiday, take some time out and see your mama well again. Then you come back and work for me again!' I saw no appeal, nor reason other than worldly concerns, to return to the world of commerce. The past four years had provided a diversion, an opportunity to see more of the world and broaden my experience of life. But there on the ridge, I was back in my element and hadn't felt so whole for years. I was connecting with something beyond myself, an inner recognition of some power encouraging me to hold to these convictions, to hold fast to the intention to lead a righteous life, something that was stable and enduring. Though I far from understood it all I was convinced I should listen to and follow my soul.

My son, preserve sound judgment and discernment ...
Then you will go on your way in safety, and your foot
*   will not stumble;*
When you lie down, you will not be afraid,
When you lie down, your sleep will be sweet.
Have no fear of sudden disaster or of the ruin that
*   overtakes the wicked,*
For the Lord will be your confidence and will keep
*   your foot from being snared.*   (Prov. 3:21, 23-26)

A sense of direction came and was met with an inner approval that brought peace, affirming the decision to resign and remain at home. A decision that previously had been made more by the heart than of the mind was now a deep confidence in the way ahead.

MEDITATION

'Seeking Direction'

Are you approaching or have you already arrived at a cross-roads in your life? A choice of what to study? Where? The type of job to go for? Whether to marry? To volunteer to do something for the first time at church? To move home, area, country? Considering a change of vocation; to go off on mission, time to retire?

There is a lot of well-meant advice. Often too much caution stops us from spreading our wings – fear of failing, shame to have got it wrong having ignored the advice. We can easily feel constricted, our style is too often cramped and we settle for the safer option, which of course could be the right option sometimes.

Better to find some space to evaluate what's in your heart and mind. Take a walk far from the madding crowd – if it's a big choice, make a day of it on your own to distil your thoughts, boil up all the advice, get rid of the steam and reduce it to its concentrated state. You won't be alone if you know the Lord. Spread all the options before Him, say them aloud, or write them out, if that helps to articulate what you're feeling and thinking, to give form to things that might seem muddled. Ask Him to speak into the clamour of advice. Heed a verse of the Bible that may come to mind. Stop to read a portion of scripture – as well as search passages that seem pertinent to your situation, allow yourself also to be led to a certain verse and meditate upon it.

Many verses address human fear and apprehension over an immediate challenge. For example, the Lord says to Joshua as he newly takes command of leading the Israelites into the Promised Land, 'Be strong and courageous, because you will lead these people to inherit the land' (Joshua 1:6). The command, 'Be strong and courageous', is repeated twice again in the same address (vv. 7 and 9), emphasising how necessary it is to counter fear.

Obedience is required if we are to know the favour and leading of the Spirit. Jesus reminds His disciples that 'If you love me, you will obey what I command' (John14:15), a statement He twice repeats in similar wording in the same passage (vv. 21 and 23). We would do well to check whether we are heeding what we're hearing in terms of putting things right as these commands are given in the context of the Counsellor – the Holy Spirit – that Jesus promised that His father would give to the disciples once they were on their own without Jesus.

At the end of the day summarise what you have been hearing – is this authentically from God or have you been frantic in trying to find too many answers – you will know by whether there has been a connection, a peace in the heart, an excitement.

> *Peace I leave with you; my peace I give you. I do not give to you as the world gives. Do not let your hearts be troubled and do not be afraid.* (John 14:27)

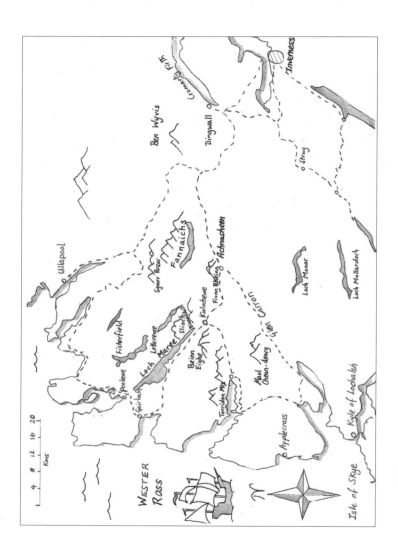

8

In Fear of Man

Slioch

Blessed are those who hunger and thirst for righteousness for they will be filled ... blessed are the pure in heart, for they will see God. (Matt. 5:6, 8)

JESUS' promise to satisfy those who seek after righteousness, says that they will in their seeking, glimpse something essentially of God. This was my desire on the summit of Ben Lawers – a pursuit that needs to be maintained with great deliberation as implied in the verse by those who 'hunger' and 'thirst'. All the certainties and convictions expressed on Ben Lawers gradually eroded over the year as I yielded to the pressure to move on from being a self-employed gardener in the Manchester area. The year had served a good purpose in seeing my mother well established and my presence and occupation back in the city that I had so consciously set out from after leaving school, had always been of a temporary nature. Surrender to the dictates of the world to improve my position in life as opposed to the noble design to opt for a purer simpler life drove me back into the business world.

Through a back-to-work programme for executives, I regained confidence to apply for jobs based on my experience and before long, had secured the position of contracts manager with a security firm in the Arabian Gulf. I sought to win approval and conform to expectations of the society in which I was raised. It reminded me years later of this warning:

Fear of man will prove to be a snare,
But whoever trusts in the Lord is kept safe.
    (Prov. 29:25)

I took advantage of a few days break before heading for the arid wastes of the Arabian Peninsula to visit the Gairloch region of North West Scotland (see 'Wester Ross' map, p. 80). Slioch is impressive with its enormous stony bastion rising above the long trough of Loch Maree separating it from the Torridon Mountains with their screes, ridges and summits of tumbling corries. The loch lay peaceful and at mid-point, a cluster of wooded islands made of more resistant matter had withstood the grinding of glaciers. Undisturbed by the loggers, magnificent remnants of the ancient Caledonian pine forest cover these islands; their massive, gnarled limbs shaped by decades of storm, speak of a heroic landscape, where bears and wolves had one-time roamed, where invading Vikings had come.

I took the usual approach to Slioch from Kinlochewe along the river flowing into the southern end of the loch before taking the path up the very steep-sided Gleann Bianasdail. The cloud-covered summit obscured an imagined view of the rocky buttresses of the Torridon range rising beyond the southern extent of long Loch Maree. I pictured a mighty wall of imposing, impenetrable rock. The wilderness of Letterewe and Fisherfield to the north-east was awe-inspiring too, although I also felt despair at ever being able to penetrate to the heart and to reach the few Munros unwilling to yield their prizes without a valiant attempt. But on my descent, emerging from the cloud base, I saw the scattered islands on Loch Maree. The sun and shadow playing over the loch turned a brief rest into a lengthy contemplation; the vastness and variety of the landscape created such an impression, made the more poignant by my imminent return to the arid wastes of the Middle East.

Although pleased to secure a new job, I wasn't thrilled to be returning to the deserts. My love of Scotland had been seriously rekindled, and the brevity of this visit only made the parting harder. Memories of forester days, hill climbs and the resolve just a year earlier on Ben Lawers to settle down to a nobler way far from the wheeling-dealing of Arab commerce haunted me all the journey south and beyond back to the Arab world. Scotland brought a strong sense of belonging. But more than that, this magnificent grandeur touched me profoundly. The scene more than inspired the soul beyond the sheer joy of looking at a superb view – this was a case of transcendence, surpassing and exceeding what could be perceived as joy from looking at a grand view. I use the term 'transcendence' as it refers to a spiritual awakening, an awareness of a divine reality beyond the outward aspect of the landscape that engages with our soul and moves us profoundly. It's as if the soul has been confronted by the otherworldliness of God. Transcendence is about spiritual experience, the inner witness, the flight of the soul that perceives something of God that is not the result of intellectual understanding, but a heartfelt conviction that sears us to the core. The grandeur pointed at something of great significance, of enduring worth, showing great power and purity. The landscape's outer appearance bore more than a suggestion of the character of the One who had made it, and like a portal, focused one's spirit on the lofty personality behind this magnificent creation. Such an encounter stops us in our tracks, takes our breath away, humbles us and brings us in awe of the artist behind such outwardly exquisite mastery. The apostle Paul writes about this witness of creation to the Creator as a first means to know God:

> *For since the creation of the world God's invisible qualities – his eternal power and divine nature – have been clearly seen, being understood from what has been made, so that men are without excuse.*   (Rom. 1:20)

Spiritual revelation

Conscious of this transcendence since the age of seventeen, it brought a sense of wonder and rapture when in the hills causing me to pause and ponder on God. But I was aware that for me this communion was limited, and depended on days like these spent in the hills, days that were very rare and precious and days that Wordsworth said came to an end in later adulthood:

> *There was a time when meadow, grove and stream,*
> *The earth, and every common sight,*
> *To me did seem*
> *Apparelled in celestial light,*

The glory and the freshness of a dream.
It is not now as it hath been of yore:
Turn whereso'er I may,
By night or day,
The things which I have seen I now can see no more.
WORDSWORTH *Ode on Immortality* [1]

What of my father's encouragement to be content with the nobler way, to seek wisdom, to journey the lesser trodden path? This surely was better for the soul, to choose to act in accordance with my authentic, true personality. I was in turmoil upon Slioch, all finer feelings were contradicted by my decision to return to the fast business world, compromised to follow the simple way of man that doesn't look beyond the purpose of life other than to earn a living. This work orientation to ensure our livelihood is a requirement that everyone has to address; but to make it our goal can very soon make it our idol. This is at the core of the 'simple ways' referred to in the proverb below. The simple way, or the materialistic centred outlook allures with its power to influence and the temptation to grow richer. It then soon becomes the measure of who we are, becoming our all-consuming preoccupation without concern for our spiritual life.

'Leave your simple ways,' spoke Wisdom 'and you will live; walk in the way of understanding'.   (Prov. 9:6)

There on Slioch my state of transcendence gave me an ability to listen, to perceive things that we are often dulled to in the

---

1. William Wordsworth, *Ode: Intimations of Immortality from Recollections of Early Childhood* (1804). Also known as *Ode, Immortality Ode* or *Great Ode* ('Poems, in Two Volumes', 1807).

busyness of life, where even leisure pursuits speak more of restlessness than of finding peace and healing and wholeness. Although these worthy inclinations echoed my father's counsel, bringing weight to the conviction, I was beginning to perceive their source as neither my own nor my father's, but to emanate from an ultimate authority. These thoughts weren't the process of my own thinking for they came forcibly from outside, in opposition to what I had neatly arranged for my next step in life and they broke in by way of revelation, overturning my petty, insignificant order and understanding.

He who forms the mountains, creates the wind,
And reveals his thoughts to man,
He who turns dawn to darkness
And treads the high places of the earth
The Lord God Almighty is his name.   (Amos 4:13)

Slioch translates from the Gaelic as 'The Spear', and while I remained on Slioch my soul was pierced as I pondered my decisions. I wanted to pursue a known ideal, but knew I was driven by a spineless decision to make something materially prestigious of my life! I returned from Slioch in denial of the higher calling, too much the coward to undo a commitment made. I felt a sense of divine disappointment, of having turned from a hand extended to me. It brought a sense of shame and a period of sorrow. Thankfully though it's not at this point that God washes His hands of us; if that were so, who would be left? It's part of His nature to be full of grace and forgiveness, going out of His way to reach us.

Jesus tells three consecutive parables in Luke chapter 15 about the state of being lost: a lost sheep, a lost coin and a wayward son. These stories were provoked by the indignation the religious people expressed when seeing Jesus eat with 'sinners' and the Lord's desire for us to know how keen He is to recover the things that are lost.

> *Suppose one of you has a hundred sheep and loses one of them. Does he not leave the ninety-nine in the open country and go after the lost sheep until he finds it? And when he finds it, he joyfully puts it on his shoulders and goes home. Then he calls his friends and neighbours together and says, 'Rejoice with me; I have found my lost sheep.'* (Luke 15:4-6)

And similarly the intent of the Lord to find someone who is lost is illustrated by the woman looking for a coin that was likely to be part of her dowry, one coin among several made into a necklace or headband that had come adrift. Her eagerness to find the coin was a frantic search made much in the same way a wife would undergo today if she had lost her wedding ring:

> *Or suppose a woman has ten silver coins and loses one. Does she not light a lamp, sweep the house and search carefully until she finds it.* (Luke 15:8)

And finally the most poignant of the three parables shows the longing of the father for the return of his wayward son, demonstrating the heart of God longing for us to come to our senses and to return contrite:

> *But while he (the wayward son) was still a long way off, his father saw him and was filled with compassion for*

him; he ran to his son, threw his arms around him and kissed him. (Luke 15:20)

God takes the initiative to find us but we are not always willing to be found just yet.

MEDITATION

'In Fear of Man'

Sometimes choices are made that don't rate among our finer moments! We bow down to other people's expectations, to the conventions of society or to the spirit of the world, driven by at least a touch of ambition, greed and pride. This can make us feel uneasy and that can sometimes be the prompting of the Spirit within.

God allows us to make mistakes – thankfully, it's not the end of the line as God works through the mistakes, even the mess. Sometimes it's the problems and the humiliation that can follow that brings us to our senses. After Jesus was arrested, Peter was recognised as one of His followers. Peter hotly denied that he knew Jesus and disowned Him three times, something the Lord had prophesied. On the third denial it says that Jesus 'turned and looked straight at Peter' (Luke 22:61), a look that undid Peter and made him recall the word the Lord had spoken to him – 'And he went outside and wept bitterly' (v. 62). Thankfully, Peter's story doesn't end there, although at the time he probably felt that he had blown it so much that there could be no restoration. In the final chapter of John's gospel we have that touching, although difficult, scene when the resurrected Lord goes to seek Peter and asks him three times, 'Do you truly love me?' – one for each denial. The public confession cancelled out the denial and Jesus' response was a three-fold declaration that Peter was to oversee the young church. That's forgiveness – God doesn't treat us as our sins deserve. There are no subclauses about God's reconciliation, no removal from the centre-play to relegate Peter (also called Simon) to the touchline. In the gospels there is so much that Jesus foresees – not just the denial, but the recognition that Peter would be a target for Satan:

> *Simon, Simon, Satan has asked to sift you as wheat. But I have prayed for you Simon that your faith might not fail. And when you have turned back, strengthen your brothers.* (Luke 22:32)

Consider a time of failure that has brought you to your spiritual senses. How did God break in/rescue you? Thank Him for His intervention and His commitment to you despite your ungodly choices. Consider how the Lord's forgiveness has brought you secure in His love to the place where you are now and be grateful for His providence.

If you're in a crisis at this moment – take hope in the Lord who can rescue you if you call on Him. You can pretend to others that you have it all together, but the Lord isn't deceived. Be honest with Him and take those first steps of changing circumstances by confessing if you've got it wrong, asking to be forgiven and then seek His strength and grace to start to make changes.

> *If we confess our sins, he is faithful and just and will forgive us our sins and purify us from all unrighteousness.* (1 John 1:9)

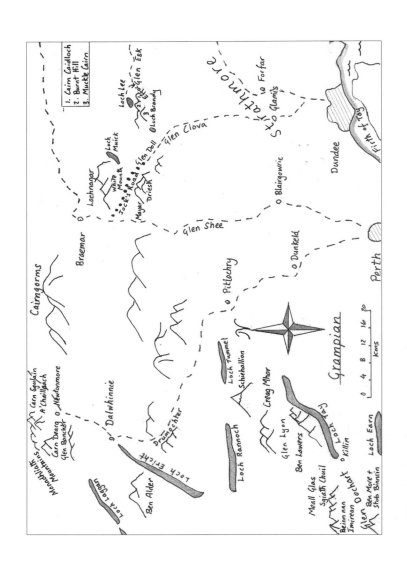

9

A Clearing of the Mists

Creag Mhor and the Glen Lyon Hills

*The path of the righteous is like the first gleam of the
  dawn,
Shining ever brighter till the full light of day.*
  (Prov. 4:18)

AFTER four years working in the Arabian Gulf, a way
opened up in 1987 to return to Scotland to run a guesthouse
in Perthshire. And here I was with Alexandra – my wife –
climbing what was at the time named 'Creag Mhor' (see
'Grampian' map, p. 90) above Perthshire's most beautiful
glen: Glen Lyon. With probably less than 200 feet of ascent
to the summit, my wife refused to go on.

It had been an ill-prepared expedition with New Zealand
friends. Initial intentions had been to do a spirited walk
above the glen with our three-month-old carried in a sling.
We made good progress on that fair day in late summer all
the way up to the high cloud line, enjoying good banter
with friends we hadn't seen for years, lured on by the fast

approaching summit of Creag Mhor, or 'Big Rock' in Gaelic. This was quite appropriate because when baby Iain had awoken he could only be pacified by a breastfeed behind the rude shelter of a big rock. Judging from the very short grass, I sensed we couldn't be far from the cloud-concealed summit. But Alexandra wasn't persuaded. I took our friends on, promising to return within fifteen minutes even if we didn't reach the summit. We walked with determination, figuring a fifteen minute wait at that altitude with a three-month-old was about as long as you would wish to leave mother and child. We were back in ten minutes having reached the summit of what would have been Alexandra's first Munro and that of our son too, if being carried up counts!

That was Alexandra's first and last Munro outing with me, the exasperated outcome of an ill-conceived trek to the summit.

This was four years on from Slioch, beyond all that inner turmoil. Dubai had proved a slippery slope. The Arab nationals being in the minority were rather inaccessible and this disappointed my hope of enjoying a social life among them that I had so enjoyed when living in Iraq. I therefore, very reluctantly, joined the British expat community, often drinking myself into oblivion to forget the hedonistic and materialistic goals – the 'simple ways' – I had stooped to, having fallen from the heights that offered true wisdom.

I met Alexandra on returning to the U.K. to be best man at a friend's wedding – an incident that rescued me – a firebrand snatched from the fire. She challenged me to read the Bible before rejecting Christianity, to exercise the same basis of judgement as I had done with other religions by reading their holy scriptures. In search of wisdom I had read the Koran and the *Bhagavad Gita* and although they had expressions of truths, neither had truly captivated me. I hadn't read the Bible because I thought it had nothing to really offer, an assumption based on sitting through chapel four times a week at a high Anglican school, where lack of conviction led to dull routines.

Like a sheep without a shepherd

After that wedding I returned to the Middle East with a Bible, instructed by Alexandra to start reading the gospels to understand something of what Christ taught and His purpose on earth. I had long evenings alone in my villa on the hillside of Jebel Ali to read, but I confess to only turning to the biblical scriptures on occasion. I admired Jesus, the one who so stood out, stood apart from any institutionalised belief, stood opposed to the religious bigots and the hypocrisy of spiritual leaders. Here was someone very radical, not fighting shy of being critical and yet at the same time a man of the people, mixing with the broken, the lowly, the undesirables, the unwell. This summary from Matthew's gospel encapsulates His humanity: 'When he saw the crowds, he had compassion upon them, because they were harassed and helpless, like sheep without a shepherd' (Matthew 9:36).

Jesus' character was especially winsome, so different from the mild, slightly effeminate figure portrayed on stained glass. Here was someone bold and manly, so unlike the way the media portray Christian ministers today.

I also warmed to Christ's followers who weren't always shown in a favourable light. These disciples had their failings written down, not to shame them but to tell the whole truth and in turn help future generations of followers to identify with their strivings and their mistakes. This transparency was refreshing when compared with the scriptures of other religions – it had an authentic ring that aroused my curiosity. I understood the claims and invitations conveyed in pithy and memorable manner in the gospels: 'I am the bread of life. He who comes to me will never go hungry' (John 6:35) – 'I am the light of the world. Whoever follows me will never walk in darkness but will have the light of life' (John 8:12).

But two things held me back. I had no big conviction of my own need, and secondly I was tired of the unhelpfulness of being labelled. Being British in the Middle East meant that new Muslim acquaintances took some time to accept me, so to say I was a believing Christian I felt would cause another huge barrier (one which I subsequently found to be unfounded as Muslims respect those who hold religious convictions more than those who are secular).

God needed to humble me. I awoke hung-over on the morning I had an important business appointment with a government minister in Abu Dhabi, someone whom I had been trying to see for months. Looking at my alarm clock I realised there wasn't enough time to make the appointment. I felt very displeased with myself and that feeling grew so much that I believe it was the work of the Spirit making me aware that I didn't have everything right, that I was unable to hold things of consequence together and highlighting my need for forgiveness.

I started reading the Acts of the Apostles and came to the part where Peter was explaining to the crowds what had just taken place at Pentecost when God poured His Spirit on His followers, giving them great boldness to declare 'the wonders of God' in a variety of languages that none of them had learned. This caused many to listen to Peter's explanation concerning who this Jesus was: '… a man accredited by God to you by miracles, wonders and signs, which God did among you through him as you yourselves know' (Acts 2:22). Peter then talked of the crucifixion followed by Jesus coming back from the dead, concluding with the statement: 'God has made this Jesus, whom you crucified, both Lord and Christ' (Acts 2:36).

Their reaction struck a chord in me as their question was my own one too.

When the people heard this, they were cut to the heart and said to Peter and the other apostles, 'Brothers, what shall we do?' (Acts 2:37)

As I read Peter's reply it seemed written as much for me as for the first-century bystanders.

Repent and be baptised every one of you in the name of Jesus Christ for the forgiveness of your sins. And you will receive the gift of the Holy Spirit. The promise is for you and your children and for all who are far off – for all the Lord will call. (Acts 2:38-39)

Feeling in great need to put my life right, I knelt and prayed, admitting my need to be forgiven, to make a clean slate of my life. In my proud independence I had messed things up and required instruction. I needed someone who I could follow not just during the rare times I was on the summits of hills, but at all times. The transaction was as simple as that and I didn't understand all the theology behind what Jesus had achieved through the cross but I took it in faith that this was something hugely necessary for Jesus' mission in the world, to give His life on the cross – not as a victim at the hands of a foreign power, or through the connivance of the religious authorities He had so outraged, but by His own freewill. Several times those authorities had tried to arrest Him but they were powerless. In reading the gospels, you see Jesus' firm purpose and control of events. Nothing was going to happen without His willing it and His execution was completing some divine mystery, that through His death He would take upon Himself the rebellion of all mankind and that there would be forgiveness for those who had walked away from God. There would be life for those who put their trust in this divine transaction.

Our pride stands in the way of accepting so gracious a gift. Often brokenness is required to produce a humility that will admit our need. It's hard to accept that we're already judged as dead, living in darkness and bound for an eternity away from God's love. Our own sense of being all right claims that we don't need such a drastic remedy to put us right with God; our doing what's right says we can make ourselves acceptable before God. If that were so then Christ's death as our substitute was totally unnecessary.

Jesus' death is past history and happened so long ago that many think it no longer relevant. It is very relevant as each will find out once we die and when we are judged by what we decided about God's Saviour. A good part of the good news of God's plan is still to come concerning the return of Christ, not as a child but as the king to end human history.

All will be called to account and His coming again will be both a joyful and a fearful thing that touches all of creation. Psalm 96 captures this well:

> *Let the heavens rejoice, let the earth be glad;*
> *Let the sea resound, and all that is in it;*
> *Let the fields be jubilant, and everything in them.*
> *Then all the trees of the forest will sing for joy;*
> *They will sing before the Lord, for he comes,*
> *He comes to judge the earth.*
> *He will judge the world in righteousness*
> *And the peoples in his truth.* (Ps. 96:11-13)

In view of this judgement, our destiny is determined by what we have decided about Christ and that is something that ought to exercise us.

I re-climbed Creag Mhor (Meall nan Aighean as it later became known with the former name relegated to a nearby subsidiary top) solo with the intention of doing the round of four summits along this fine horseshoe. Reflecting on all the good things that had happened since those destructive days of meaninglessness in Dubai when it seemed I had given up on the pursuit of wisdom, I recognised that One hadn't given up on me. My tendency for spiritual reflection upon the hills was inspired by their Maker seeking a relationship with me, stimulating a dialogue. I came to understand that Wisdom wasn't an inanimate concept but a person. This is what is written about Wisdom personified:

> *The Lord brought me forth as the first of His works,*
> *before his deeds of old; I was appointed from eternity,*

from the beginning, before the world began. When there were no oceans, I was given birth, when there were no springs abounding with water; before the mountains were settled in place, before the hills, I was given birth, before he made the earth or its fields or any of the dust of the world. I was there when he set the heavens in place, when he marked out the horizon on the face of the deep, … Then I was the craftsman at his side. I was filled with delight day after day, rejoicing always in his presence, rejoicing in his whole world and delighting in mankind. (Prov. 8:22-31)

This personification of Wisdom, this notion of co-deity, this shadowy figure from ancient scriptures, of one in accord with the Creator at the beginning is revealed in the New Testament as the 'Word':

In the beginning was the Word, and the Word was with God and the Word was God. He was with God in the beginning. Through him all things were made; without him nothing was made that has been made. In him was life and that life was the light of men. The light shines in the darkness, but the darkness has not understood it. John 1:1-5.

And the Word is not just a personification, 'The Word became flesh and made his dwelling among us' (v. 14). The Word became a person. Concerning the coming of Christ into the world, the evangelist John says, 'We have seen his glory, the glory of the One and only, who came from the Father, full of grace and truth' (John 1: 14). The Word was and is Jesus.

The real dawn

The mist had cleared. A few solitary ascents into the hills had enabled me to peep above the cloud cover and on to heaven and to understand. Seeing beyond physical nature and comprehending something of the person behind the creation, I began to see One who is pure and all-powerful, who is indeed the beginning of wisdom. The real dawn came in realising that the Creator wasn't some distant, awesome force, but one who sought me in each of those breakthrough experiences upon the heights, and latterly in the depths. The person who came into our history as a man to show exceptional compassion and power and who made the supreme statement of love by dying in our place that we might have life in all its fullness.

I have come that they may have life, and have it to the full. (John 10:10)

David Henderson – the minister at Glamis – had befriended me one day back in the time when I was a forester. Our encounter had been brought about when I had been working in the tree nursery adjacent to his manse. Hearing about my love of hillwalking and of reading literature, he invited me to the manse where I became an occasional visitor. Our talks ranged from his reminiscences of war years in North Africa and the Middle East and other reflections of a traveller, to sharing classical music that expanded my limited knowledge. We also discussed things of a spiritual nature. During spiritual discussions David was never pushy, giving me the freedom to express and explore some of my own searching for meaning which he would helpfully comment upon and occasionally point me to appropriate scriptures. He gifted me a Bible and inscribed on the inside cover this:

For your future meditations on the mountains –
and then quoted the metrical version of Psalm 40:2:

He took me from a fearful pit,
And from the miry clay,
And on a rock he set my feet,
Establishing my way.

Indeed my way had been especially slippery from which I seemed incapable of extricating myself until God rescued me, setting my feet upon the firmness of a rock. The psalm goes on to say, 'He put a new song in my mouth, a hymn of praise to my God' (40:3). To praise the Creator rather than the creation became much more personal and meaningful – an expression that could happen at any time and at any place, not dependent on being in the hills.

MEDITATION

'A Clearing of the Mists'

Life can be like ascending a high ridge in wind-swept cloud, of walking precariously across shifting screes. Then comes the breakthrough moment when the clouds part momentarily and you see down into the valley as well as to the far horizon and sight wonderful things that make you stop to marvel and to praise.

Consider your own conversion moment when the clouds parted and you saw clearly and it all made sense, and yet like a far-reaching panorama we can only take in as much as a short look can retain. What were the things that brought clarity that ceased your objections?

Articulate what happened, the scriptures that God particularly used to bring you to this point of conviction? Seek to reduce it to a five minute summary of how the mists cleared for you and share this with someone. Pray that you will be led to think of someone to share this with and pray that God will use your testimony to help clear the mists in that person's life. Don't be dismayed by the name of the one the Lord brings to mind, thinking they won't listen or will just scoff. Consider Ananias in Damascus who God called to go to see Saul:

> *'Lord,' Ananias answered, 'I have heard many reports about this man and all the harm he has done to your saints in Jerusalem. And he has come here with authority from the chief priests to arrest all who call on your name.'*
>
> *But the Lord said to Ananias, 'Go! This man is my chosen instrument to carry my name before the Gentiles and their kings and before the people of Israel.'*
> (Acts 9:13-15)

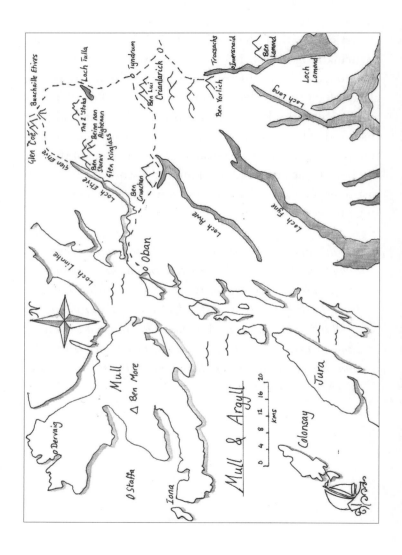

Mull & Argyll

10

Impetuosity Checked

Ben Lomond

MY father had been instrumental in mapping out a solo trip for me when I moved to Scotland to take up forestry; the route was an upland version of the West Highland Way. Having just finished my secondary education, I was desperate to find some space and restoration in the hills.

The train arrived early afternoon on the southern shores of Loch Lomond (see 'Mull and Argyll' map, p. 102). Being mid-summer, plenty of daylight remained to get beyond the town and on to the quiet road near the east shore of the Loch. My first objective was Ben Lomond and then to continue north over the coming fortnight, up the length of the Loch, over the hills west of Crianlarich, on to Glen Coe, ending the outward journey with a crossing over the Mamores to ascend Ben Nevis (see 'Lochaber' map, p. 124, for the continuation sheet north). The route then headed south on a parallel course east of the outward route, culminating in the Trossachs. There was a real spring in my step approaching this herculean undertaking, elated at leaving England behind, bursting with excitement at completing my studies and full of anticipation at coming to a country of wide open spaces. All this coupled with the fine prospect of moving to this wonderful land to work meant I was in high spirits.

The evening weather was changeable bringing an early dusk halfway up Ben Lomond. Determined to travel light, I had only a survival bag to sleep in. With rain on the wind, I chose to lie on the leeward side of a mature spruce forest. Finishing the last sandwich of the day, I put on every item of clothing I had and bedded down, feeling unnerved by the lack of shelter and the absence of a companion to bolster morale. Longing for the idea of time out on my own, I hadn't anticipated feeling like this! No sooner had I settled down the midges came, signalling my presence to all their minions in the area! They were bothersome to the extreme. Voracious for blood, they made sleep impossible for a long while as I vainly tried to protect myself, swatting away many crawling over my face, driven at times to frantic face slapping. Eventually, demoralised and worn out, I yielded in the fight, and fell asleep only to be awakened later by rain on my face. Even whilst it rained, the midges didn't let up. The night wore on with more showers. Again I grew troubled by the loneliness of my situation, disenchanted by this all too basic nature of extreme camping. The survival bag did what it said – I survived; unlike the sleeping-bag in which you normally have a good night's rest. I emerged the following morning very damp from the chronic condensation that had formed inside the plastic bag.

I was on my way with a sense of relief as a grey dawn emerged out of the gloom, glad of the wind beyond the forest to scatter the midge infestation that had caused my hands and face to become especially swollen. Ben Lomond was unmemorable, shrouded in mist and I was down at the hotel at Inversnaid in time for breakfast having already walked some 11 kilometres. The company of people, irrespective of not speaking with anyone, restored my spirits as much as did a full-cooked breakfast. I was in no hurry to push on, but loitered, enjoying this small hive of human activity. On many subsequent occasions I have found I'm better content with my fellow man after a time of solitude, more at one with the world and glad to engage.

Learning the hard way

Eventually I prised myself free and continued northwards, walking in a very idle fashion punctuated by frequent rests. By mid-evening I passed the top of the loch and continued up river to choose a suitable spot to wade across – top-of-the-thigh deep. This is not a recommended way to end a day before camping in a survival bag without a change of clothing. Having spoken with my father from the public phone at Inversnaid he advised camping above 2,000 feet in a bid to outdo the midges. It seemed every midge in the area had homed in again with great tenacity and it's perhaps hard to believe how something so small could drive you so demented. Still wet from the river crossing and therefore concerned about the night-time cold above 2,000 feet, I lacked the sangfroid to follow my father's advice and favouring an easily accessible sheltered place I camped too low down. The midge despair and the lack of sleep for a second night, put things out of perspective. Added to that was the recurrence of that unexpected sense of haunting loneliness. My will to push on north was crushed by the prospect of being devoured through a third sleepless night.

The zeal for escaping to the Scottish hills, ill-equipped for camping had got the better of me and now I was paying the consequences. Years later I was reminded of this very venture when reading this Proverb:

> *It is not good to have zeal without knowledge,*
> *Nor to be hasty and miss the way.* (Prov. 19:2)

Learning the hard way is to heed a lesson none the less. I believe such mistakes made in the hills have forced me not only to be wiser in better preparation for future trips but in life too, to better anticipate what some of the challenges and obstacles might be if I were to make a certain choice and to adequately prepare for what could be required. Whilst zeal is a necessary ingredient to spur us on, to give us motivation to set about a task, it needs to be put on hold whilst we draw up a check list to realise the venture. When we can add to that the knowledge that comes from experience, a knowledge that's often enhanced by talking it through with those who have travelled that way themselves, we are more likely to succeed in life's ventures.

These lessons came home to me when just one day into a new job I realised that the direction it was taking me wasn't ideal. What had seemed good at the time because it was a job that rescued me from the slough of being unemployed, on reflection led to where I had no desire to go and my mother encouraged me to quit. Later another job that I liked the look of didn't seem to fit my capabilities until I calmly assessed what I had to offer by drawing on previous experience. Reassured that I did meet some of the requirements, I felt encouraged to apply. At this I was successful.

I rolled up my survival bag with difficulty as my fingers ached and had become almost unpliable due to the fantastical swelling from all the bites making my knuckles unrecognisable. Midges were plastered so densely they effectively camouflaged the lurid orange of the bag. At least I had this proof to show my father who was likely to be disappointed by my only reaching just beyond Loch Lomond. I put out my thumb to hitch to Glasgow and felt it most fortuitous when the first passing vehicle stopped – a lorry bound for Glasgow.

I was too young, inexperienced and easily disheartened on my own, although I would never minimise the effect of a midge infestation. I had been foolishly ill-prepared through my gung-ho approach to travelling with minimal possessions. Idealistic about wild adventure, a lesson was learned the hard way. But perhaps that is the only way to counter the swagger of youth, although it prevented me from repeating the same mistakes for a time at least. This was all part of growing up, of taking responsibility, of recognising the need to practically learn and gain wisdom in life.

Have two goals: wisdom – that is, knowing and doing right – and common sense. Don't let them slip away, for they will fill you with living energy, and bring you honour and respect. (Prov. 3:21-22 THE LIVING BIBLE)

When I did attempt overnight camping trips in the hills much more latterly, it was with a tent, a home to crawl into that took away that sense of alienation, kept me out of reach of the midge and made one thankful for the simple gift of shelter and basic provisions to snack upon. I also learned it's much easier to endure difficulties when shared with others. Decades later, a group of us had gambled on some late winter camping hoping to catch one of the milder spells we had been enjoying in the days leading up to our departure. But the day we set off, it snowed all across Scotland and a storm kept the ferries in port. Everyone in our small party put on such a brave face when we settled down for the night that morale was kept up almost till morning, when frozen-limbed we stumbled out into fresh snow. The experience would have been quite different on your own. The camaraderie from being in it together, created a great talking point in the days that followed.

MEDITATION

'Impetuosity Checked'

Enthusiasm is a great motivator, but too much enthusiasm without adequate preparation can prove disastrous.

If enthusiasm has ever got the better of you, do you still have it? Or have you reduced everything to cold logic and lost the drive to do daring exploits? Have you become a know-it-all and done-it-all? Do you clip the wings of others, especially your children, so they cease to fly? Of course we can caution others, but if it's at the expense of being so critical of another's attempt to rise off the ground in a first tentative flight then we need to seriously reconsider. We would do well to recognise that making mistakes is the fast track to learning at times; an unforgettable experience of failing is a constant reminder to prepare better.

How can you use your 'knowing-better' attitude to be creative in helping someone towards achieving rather than pulling them down?

And if your enthusiasm is spent, better take a fresh look at where it went. How can you recover it? Recapture the young person that still exists somewhere within. Recovering enthusiasm is vital in our ability to relate to a new generation. Showing a readiness to trust is essential to help another rise off the ground and having an open and generous spirit to see the opportunities more than the possible failures.

Look at Acts 11:19-26. Here was a strange and new thing happening, a church made up of not only Jews but Greeks as well. Consider how this will have been viewed by the conservative Jews back at the epicentre in Jerusalem? The inclusion of Gentiles (non-Jews) into the church at Antioch was radical. Consider how a heavy-handed approach might have looked. However, Barnabas, the Son of Encouragement, was thankfully sent – note his credentials in verse 23. He was a man who saw the evidence of the grace and favour of God (vv. 21 and 23) and the Lord used Barnabas to bring in an even greater harvest (end of v. 24). Clearly here was someone prepared to be broad in his acceptance of others and give people an opportunity rather than allow prejudice to jaundice his view. Consider how Barnabas alone out of all the disciples was prepared to meet with the one-time persecutor of the church, Saul, to verify whether he had been truly converted as he claimed to be (see Acts 9: 26-27). What an open mind and heart! And now in this harvest time in Antioch, Barnabas realised he needed a special helper and remembered Saul back in his not so distant home town of Tarsus. Saul was untested but Barnabas had obviously seen enough to like him and to take the risk of bringing him there to teach the new disciples.

Can you identify someone to bring alongside you in a task?

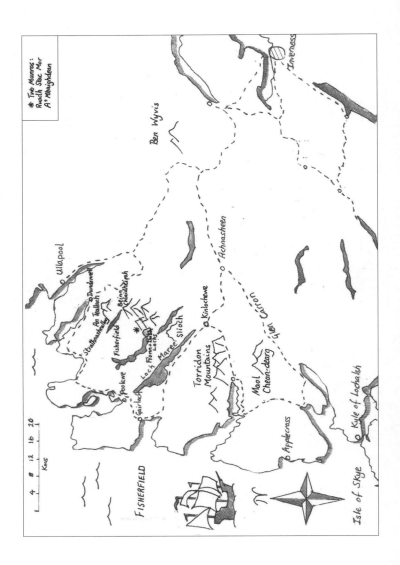

* Two Munros:
Ruadh Stac Mor
A' Mhaighdean

Ben Wyvis

Ullapool

Dundonnell

Strathnasheelag

Beinn Dearg

Fisherfield

Loch Maree

Poolewe

Loch Fionn Loch

Sloch

Gairloch

Kinlochewe

Torridon Mountains

Achnasheen

Glen Carron

Maol Chean-dearg

Applecross

Kyle of Lochalsh

Isle of Skye

Inverness

FISHERFIELD

Kms
4 8 12 16 20

11

Epic Exploits

Fisherfield and Letterewe

THE mountain bike was ready for the rigours of the track ahead. My son had gifted me this fine bike for Christmas when he was only fifteen, saved for from his meagre earnings from a paper round and without doubt this remains the most touching present I've ever received. Four distant Munros were the objective that day, a round trip of 38.5 kilometres and a total climb of 2,110 metres. This expedition was categorised as being among the elite few that I had pondered for years, not daring to embark on it as I questioned my ability to tackle the task.

I set off just before dawn in late August having camped the night in the car near Dundonnell (see 'Fisherfield' map, p. 112). The ascent was tough, not only due to the persistent gradient of over three kilometres, but also due to the broken nature of the track with so much loose and large debris making traction difficult on a bike. At the other end of the day, exhausted as the last light faded fast, the rubble-strewn track frustrated travelling at any speed along the lengthy downhill stretch.

At this early morning hour the cloud hung over the tops of the cliff bastions of An Teallach to the west, rendering them dark, uninviting and 'off-limits'. The pass was reached in a sweat, rewarded by a glimpse of the first of the distant prizes that day: Beinn a'Chlaidheimh (subsequently downgraded from Munro status after being remeasured and found lacking by some foot or such like). This peak lies towards the northern end of a remote ridge deep in the hinterland between five ancient forests: Dundonnell, Strathnasheallag, Fisherfield, Letterewe and Kinlochewe. With a majestic sweep of high ridge, two further peaks rose and a third hidden from view lay distant, separated from the main ridge. This was the half-way point to the day's epic undertaking – some fourteen kilometres as the crow flies from where I had stopped my bike at the pass!

A long fast sweep down the track brought me in no time to the strath below. A late starter at using a bike on these long hauls, I was glad to cover the monotonous way along tracks in quick time. Using the bike would have shortened the time considerably on the lengthy excursions to some of the Cairngorm summits from Deeside. However, there were some drawbacks. Once down in the strath, the fine track terminated into a muddy path making further progress so troublesome that the bike was soon abandoned behind a rocky outcrop. A swollen river had to be waded, the swift torrent lapping halfway up my thighs threatened to topple me from an insecure footing among the shifting stones of the river bed. Then began the unrelenting slog to the peak, steepening at the final section. The approach to and the ascent of the first hill is usually the hardest part of the day, invariably demanding the lion's share of the time and effort making you question whether you've bitten off more than you can chew. At that moment you long for a second wind to kick in, a rhythm to develop, aided by the sweeping ridges and giving in my opinion the best in hillwalking. That mechanical, almost unconscious progress means you can appreciate the views whilst moving, lifting the spirit when thoughts can develop uninterrupted, often bringing a more sustained dialogue with God.

The majesty of hills seen for the first time, like that first sighting on this trek of A' Mhaighdean and Ruadh Stac Mor to the west inspire a pioneering wonder. Anticipation of this moment had led to me studying the Ordnance Survey sheet of this area on many a night back home with childlike wonder; a beautiful sheet which I had splayed out entire across the floor with its tightening knots of browns tracing sinewy contours of rugged peaks ringed with desperate corries and great shoots of screes in vast interiors, punctuated by the expansive blues of lochs with a prevailing pattern running south-east to north-west as if bound by some mysterious law. This aesthetically pleasing map is topped off by the deeply indented coastline with its sandy bays and rocky windswept promontories from Ullapool to Gairloch and the exquisite ancient Caledonian pine forests of Loch Maree's islands; all of these spectacular features raising anticipation of great adventures ahead. The imaginary journey made safely cocooned in the warmth of home on a winter's night is fantastic, the landscapes visualised, the terrain anticipated. To view far-reaching ridge systems and remote windswept lochs making up vast hinterlands, bold and rugged, creates a huge sense of awe. The remote Munros present enormous challenges, often without paths, the domain of huge herds of red mountain deer that dissolve as soon as they scent your presence, impressing all the more a sense of grand isolation. These aren't hills that can easily be ticked off; they require careful preparation if you're not to be defeated in the giving of your all.

Striving for the heroic and epic

Fourteen months later I tackled the Fisherfield Munros that had been tantalisingly sighted from the first great bike excursion. Again my mountain bike made this epic trip manageable in the shorter daylight hours in October, approaching from sea level at Poolewe. The first five kilometres along a well-defined Land Rover track were done in the dark to facilitate this gargantuan round trip of forty-one kilometres, ensuring that the more complex part navigationally fell within daylight hours. What started as a firm surface deteriorated into a rough road and then a forest track rising on to a broad massif. This made for easy going along what had become a path, providing far-reaching views of Fionn Loch and the rugged wastes beyond. The approach led to the novelty of negotiating a causeway crossing a substantial isthmus between Fionn and Dubh lochs.

The dangers of its isolation were impressed upon me by meeting a lone female hiker who hadn't seen anyone for two days. Anxious to tell her near fatal tale, she rolled up her trouser leg to reveal a blood-soaked cloth around a swollen knee. The previous day whilst descending along the precipitous edge of Ruadh Stac Mor, a great and sudden gust of wind nearly took her over the cliffs. Falling to her knees to prevent what would have been sure death over the edge, the wind snatched one of her walking poles, hurling it over the ledge beside her. It was a heart-stopping moment and she bore the bloodied and bruised consequences. As her route lay along my return leg, we agreed that should she be unable to complete the distance, she was to pitch her tent and get into her sleeping-bag and I would help her on my return. It was a decision I rued all day, I should have forfeited my climb towards those two elusive Munros to help a fellow walker. I reasoned that she was intrepid and doubted whether she would have agreed to my accompanying her when still capable of limping along at a reasonable rate. Still I could have magnanimously made the offer! The fact I didn't see her on my return was testament to her gritty resolve. My own doggedness showed that the Munros had become an obsession that needed to be checked.

Several outings within ten days of one another can physically and mentally hone you and yet the sombre sense of trepidation, unsure of how you are going to fare, of whether you will succeed or be forced into submission, nags away relentlessly. A healthy dose of apprehension helps you prepare better. Invariably I always achieved what I had set out to do on these epic walks, but I have known defeat, not by demanding distances, but from some climbs of technical complexity in adverse weather conditions.

A completed expedition produces a mixture of humility (humbled by the energy spent) and of pride in overcoming the intimidation that such a hike had long exerted. Is it audacious and foolhardy to tackle so remote and long distance a walk on your own, to resist the sometime urge to cut your losses and head for home? It's certainly character building. And perhaps without these challenges we are lesser people, more timid and indecisive. To not step up to the mark and to not take up the challenge, detracts from what we can be and makes us settle for the lesser, the unremarkable. Does a desire to keep only to the all too familiar in life, contribute to a growing dullness about us? Do we breed a preoccupation about and place a growing importance on sundry matters which numb the ear of the listener? Maintaining the mundane round of existence makes some seek escape through drink, drugs and sex in pursuit of some transcendence or other authentic experience.

Our safety obsessed era and nanny-state policies stamp on the daring urge, making us shadows of our real inner selves that strive at times for something heroic and epic. 'Is there an element of risk?' seems to be the tantamount concern that has us quitting before even setting out. Such thinking makes 'cowards of us all' and creates unfulfilled longings that fester and no doubt lead to pent up frustrations. A man like King David, although never perfect, was trained by God through great challenge and adversity. It is to such examples as David – and other heroes of the faith – that we should aspire and compare ourselves to, not to one another. His trials were opportunities to realise God's power and made him declare:

> *It is God who arms me with strength and makes my*
> *   way perfect.*
> *He makes my feet like the feet of a deer;*
> *He enables me to stand on the heights....*
> *Your right hand sustains me; you stoop down to make*
> *   me great.*
> *You broaden the path beneath me,*
> *So that my ankles do not turn over.*
> *   (Ps. 18:32-33, 35-36)*

In terms of enterprises of faith, the spirit of this age demands everything has to be planned to the minutest detail and only when risk-assessed and adequately resourced, will it get the backing of the committee. This is quite contrary to the life of faith we're called to. Hudson-Taylor commented, 'Unless there is an element of risk in our exploits for God, there is no need for faith.' Faith in essence is about risk taking, of being ready to step beyond human resources to trust God, knowing that He will provide the means and open the way to enable us to succeed in His plans. The key is to hold in tension with one another the need to plan as well as to hold on to faith. Faith demands that we follow the prompting of the word and the Spirit as God directs, not to waver in doubt and therefore to never step forward.

Bowing to this nanny-led age, we remain spiritual dwarfs. Where are the Davids of our age? Where is the spirit that dares us to set out on exploits? Where's the desire to spiritually train to seek the glory of God, to know His equipping? Where's the drive that had Paul say:

Suffering produces perseverance; perseverance, character; and character, hope. And hope does not disappoint us, because God has poured out his love into our hearts by the Holy Spirit, whom he has given us. (Rom. 5:3-5)

Perhaps because we have a diminutive view of God's greatness we don't consider He will delight in strengthening our arm in matters of great enterprise and walk with us the great heights where few dare to tread.

There are some good hill starters to psych you up for the truly epic, such as the parallel ridges flanking Glen

Shiel where as many as seven Munros can be walked in a day without great difficulty and much satisfaction. Accomplishing these outings helps you prepare for the ultimate walks into Fisherfield, Letterewe and Knoydart, and even the Cairngorms when climbing four or five remote summits in a day. These challenge the limits of endurance and consign such exploits to the stuff of legend among our personal memoirs, causing us to reflect on epic enterprises with a twinkle in the eye when the strength of youth is past. Tackling such remote Munros in a day makes you question whether you're really capable. You mentally go from, 'No, I can't do it,' to 'Well, it might just be possible.' You figure out that if you're to prepare by walking other treks of increasing altitude and distance, then you bring the epic exploit into the realms of possibility. Unsure of success and not minimising the challenge, you go resolute, prayerful, with a face set as a flint and without trace of misplaced bravado.

Great reward

The reward is indeed great. Vast tracts of new hill country is explored for the first time, a whole map crossed in a single outing, lochs you never knew the existence of sighted: great ten-mile long lochs with names you've never heard, some so hard to pronounce that they remain nameless in your head yet indelibly imprinted on your memory. Truly awesome is sighting a loch set in magnificent isolation, materialising out of the parting mists for brief but magical moments; its huge expanse observed from some craggy promontory of a beetling ridge. There's the intrepid thrill of walking where there are no paths, wading river crossings for lack of a bridge, treading printless snow, crossing swaths of peat morass without trace of human passage, of reaching summits whose very small cairns speak of how infrequently these remote summits are visited.

It's quite an adventure to walk a twelve-hour day and not to see another soul. The challenge to haul yourself up the final pass to reach the homeward stretch taxes every muscle and causes you to plunge deep within to summon the commitment to press on despite the great desire to collapse. This determination causes you to summon the strength to complete the route persevering in prayer that God will help you through what has become a great ordeal. Afterwards comes the genuine thankfulness that your life was preserved, that the Lord enabled. These are lessons that steel us for other exploits in life. Refusing to cower before a heap of scaring statistics, of setting your face against the odds, of making yourself deaf to the well-meant advice that it can't be done or shouldn't be tackled, of not giving up until all is done. And yet you still need to calculate, to assess, and train to work up for the big feat. You need to make light of the standards of the over-circumspect by training the bold eye of faith and to hold to convictions. It's the keeping of the prize before you that helps us to persevere and this is so true of the spiritual life that caused Paul to reflect, 'I consider that our present sufferings are not worth comparing with the glory that will be revealed in us' (Rom. 8:18).

MEDITATION

'Epic Exploits'

There are some Munros that raise the stakes and demand that you work on your fitness and stamina in a progressive

121

programme. This chapter's theme is about daring to tackle the epic which in the spiritual life requires faith.

How do you respond to a challenge of something you enjoy? This could be progressively working through music grades to become adept at playing an instrument; working up distances to run a marathon; writing a book; developing a series of drawings/paintings on a theme; learning another language; a DIY building project bigger than previously attempted.

Do you see the hugeness of the task and give up before you've begun, overwhelmed? 'A journey of a thousand miles is started by a single step.' Sometimes we just need to begin, be committed to that first footstep and tentatively go about achieving the epic project.

Some give up before truly beginning, or if they fall don't get up to run the race but settle for something less. King David's trials were opportunities to realise God's power and made him declare:

I sought the Lord, and he answered me;
He delivered me from all my fears.
Those who look to him are radiant;
Their faces are never covered with shame.
This poor man called, and the Lord heard him;
He saved him out of all his troubles. (Ps. 34:4-6)

We can sense the joy of David's breakthrough, we can catch hold of the freedom of lifting off the brake of our own limitations and doubts to allow God to direct, to enable and lead us through to be overcomers. Let us be inspired by this testimony which David was eager to share.

Is there something on your heart that you would like to begin? Has there been a spiritual prompting to do so? Have you tried before and failed? What's stopping you from learning from the experience and giving it another go?

What has God been challenging you to consider? Taking on a new ministry you've never tried before? To learn to trust again after you've been seriously let down? The need to extend the same forgiveness to others as God has shown to you and to get beyond a stifling bitterness? There's a first for everyone, an opportunity to prove God's equipping and sustaining hand. ... Will you dare take that first step? Ask for the Lord's help.

The angel of the Lord encamps around those who fear
  him,
And he delivers them.
Taste and see that the Lord is good;
Blessed is the man who takes refuge in him.
Fear the Lord, you his saints,
For those who fear him lack nothing.
The lions may grow weak and hungry,
But those who seek the Lord lack no good thing.
  (Ps. 34:7-10)

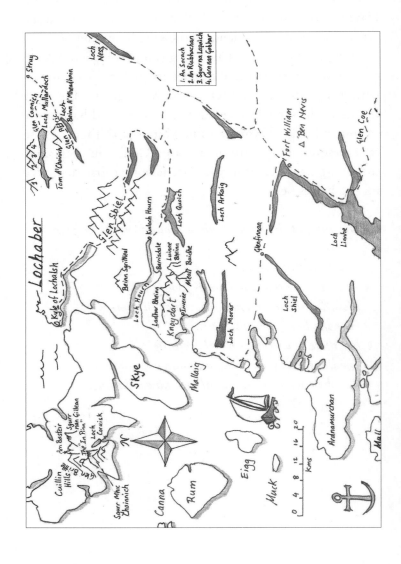

Lochaber

1. An Socach
2. An Riabhachan
3. Sgurr na Lapaich
4. Carn nan Gobhar

Loch Ness

Glen Cannich   Strey
Loch Mullardoch
Glen Affric   Loch-
Beinn A'Mheadhoin
Tom A'Choinich

Glen Shiel

Beinn Sgritheal
Kinloch Hourn
Loch Quoich
Loch Arkaig

Fort William
△ Ben Nevis

Glen Coe

Kyle of Lochalsh

Loch Hourn
Barrisdale
Ladhar Bheinn
Kneydart   Luinne Bheinn
Inverie   Meall Buidhe

Loch Morar

Glenfinnan

Loch Shiel

Loch Linnhe

Skye

Cuillin Hills
An Bastier
Sgurr nan Gillean
"The In Pinn"
Loch Coruisk
Sgurr Mhic Choinnich

Mallaig

Canna

Rum

Eigg

Muck

Ardnamurchan

Mull

0 4 8 12 16 20
Kms

12

Placing Your Trust

The Inaccessible Pinnacle, the Skye Cuillin

HILLWALKERS I've met and accounts I've read tend to celebrate the Cuillin peaks (see 'Lochaber' map, p. 124) as the ultimate in hillwalking in Britain. In terms of challenge, I most definitely agree. But as for beauty and majesty, I have many other preferences. I sense though that I'm in a minority. Climbing Sgurr nan Gillean, the second of the Cuillins I climbed, made me extremely wary. Maybe it's the adrenaline rush that thrills some, which as a solo walker makes me so preoccupied as to take away the pleasure. I had tried to descend the steep ridge down from Sgurr nan Gillean to Am Basteir – 'The Executioner' – and needing to avoid the ridge top that breaks into a series of splintered chimney stacks, I took to what seemed a good wide ledge on the west side. As I sidled along it narrowed above a tremendous yawning drop. Before long, I had only a toe-hold, a point reached with much lip-biting, hoping that the ledge would broaden. But that was wishful thinking and I had come too far. I thought of my wife and children, the latter being just one and three years old at the time, and realised that I no longer lived for myself. I slowly edged my way back, fairly terrified at how close I had come to death. I had allowed bravado and stoic determination to take me a step too far. I was reminded of the Proverb:

Pride goes before destruction,
A haughty spirit before a fall. (Prov. 16:18)

Sometimes wisdom dictates that we make a judgement call, when prudence gets the better of misplaced valour. This seems to be contradictory to what was shared in the previous chapter about the need to persevere and to overcome the odds. It takes wisdom, which often comes with experience, to discern between driven perseverance and all-out pride.

The Cuillins are complex in places, perhaps better tackled alongside those who intimately know the routes and who could have told me that the reasonable ledge I had started out along towards 'The Executioner' eventually terminated. The gabbro rock along some ridges is magnetic, rendering a compass useless. Rising on this edge of the Atlantic, the Cuillins form much cloud and have more than their fair share of lousy weather. This often reduces visibility to such an extent that you wish you could depend on the compass readings especially with cliffs abounding.

Eventually I made ascents of most of the Cuillin, with only two remaining, the In Pinn (as the Inaccessible Pinnacle is colloquially referred to) and Sgurr Mhic Choinnich – the only hill with a Gaelic name I can always recall as it proved to be my nemesis. It took six outings in total to complete just these two!

A reliable guide

The In Pinn requires a mountaineering friend or guide to safely scale the 150 foot fin of rock mounted precariously near the rounded top of Sgurr Dearg. The rock climb is classified only as 'moderate' and technically presents no difficulty. It's the exposure that intimidates, testing nerves as the mountain falls precipitously three thousand feet below into the grey turbulence of Loch Coruisk. I had previously come to the base of the In Pinn during a long ridge walk; the rocky pinnacle denied me the summit, but impressed upon me the need for a guide. Twice I made arrangements with one guide, driving the four hour journey from Central Scotland, only to meet or have a call from the guide saying the ascent was called off due to it being too wet or too windy. Since that was all too frequent on Skye I opted for a different guide. My new guide gave me much confidence as he trained the SAS in winter mountaineering in Switzerland and the two of us set off with another hillwalker needing assistance. The wind speeds were unfavourable and before reaching the ridge top, we made a lengthy stop in a sheltered spot waiting for the wind to slacken which according to the forecast it would. We waited a long time and maybe the wind speed had dropped a little, although not obviously so, when we proceeded the final few hundred feet to the top of the ridge subdued in cloud.

The Inaccessible Pinnacle suddenly materialised from out of the torn, battle grey clouds, dark and sheer, utterly menacing, making you feel instantly insignificant and quite unequal to the task. The top of the fin was lost in a whirlwind of swirling cloud, ethereal, and seemingly impregnable. This was a rare place, somewhere no-one should have the audacity or the presumption to approach. Its appearance, and the thoughts and feelings it inspired, brought to mind a couple of consecutive Psalms.

> *The Lord made the heavens. Splendour and majesty are*
> *   before him;*
> *Strength and glory are in his sanctuary …*
> *Worship the Lord in the splendour of his holiness;*
> *Tremble before him all the earth.*
> *Clouds and thick darkness surround him;*
> *Righteousness and justice are the foundation of his*
> *   throne …*
> *His lightning lights up the world;*
> *The earth sees and trembles.*
> *The mountains melt like wax before the Lord, before*
> *   the Lord of all the earth.*
> *The heavens proclaim his righteousness, and all the*
> *   peoples see his glory.*   (Ps. 96:5-6, 9; Ps. 97:2, 4-6)

The spectacle was truly transcendent, contrasting my own finite, frail and inconsequential person with the grandeur that is the Lord's. How audacious to be too familiar with the Lord! It brings to mind the way the Lord revealed himself on Mount Sinai:

> *On the morning of the third day there was thunder and*
> *lightning, with a thick cloud over the mountain, and a*
> *very loud trumpet blast. Everyone in the camp trembled*

128

... Mount Sinai was covered with smoke, because the Lord descended on it in fire. The smoke billowed up from it like smoke from a furnace, the whole mountain trembled violently, and the sound of the trumpet grew louder and louder. (Exod. 19:16-19)

We should encounter the Lord with awe and wonder, in a sense of needing to remove our shoes as we approach hallowed ground. And how amazing that His favour is extended to the likes of me, that I am not instantly consumed.

At this point had the guide said it was too risky to climb, I would have happily descended without a word, relieved even to part with my money for the day. Instead he said:

'Now then, I don't want any whingeing from either of you,' our once affable guide suddenly barked at us, transformed from being a very pleasant companion to some stern drill sergeant. 'These are borderline conditions – wind speed thirty miles per hour – any stronger, it wouldn't be safe to go. We're going to get up quickly. I don't care how you climb – forget finesse, just get up, using knees and elbows if you have to. I'll be keeping you on a tight rope and I won't stop short of pulling you up if I have to.'

He appointed me to climb first up the very edge of the rock fin once he had ascended and had belayed on halfway up, out of sight and barely within ear-shot. He had explained that I was to feed the rope behind me into a shallow crevice running like a seam down the edge of the fin so that if my companion slipped, the rope would remain taut in the crevice and prevent him from getting battered at high speed from a lengthy pendulum swing across one side of the rock fin. A move that could prove potentially fatal.

The summit

The ascent wasn't difficult, but this kind of talk and the grim hostility of the weather and this insane giant hand of rock kept you in a constant state of heightened agitation. Then the summit was reached. With the visibility reduced to about thirty feet it made it impossible to see the main bulk of the mountain below us. No cause for celebration as we had yet to abseil down, lean out and walk an unknown rock to an unsighted base. Just as I was getting used to abseiling after a forty year break from school days and showing signs of some finesse, one final push brought me ungainly on to my bottom at the base of the fin.

It was all over very quickly just as our guide had dictated and we picked our way across large rock slabs and other boulder intrusions on this much scarred mountain ridge. Emerging from the cloud and seeing the green of the glen below broke the tension and for the first time I began to appreciate that we had ascended the feared In Pinn that had thwarted me on so many occasions. Relieved, I had determined beforehand that this would be my last attempt on the In Pinn. With all the expense and frustration of previous visits being called off I had decided that the challenge had become an obsession that just had to be dropped. I had prepared myself to be one of those fellows who had climbed all the Munros except the In Pinn, as is true of Sir Hugh Munro who ascended all but this one. I had prepared to just settle for that, refusing the 'just have to' attitude of ticking every summit off the list. And there are some Munroists who have climbed all except one, reluctant to have their name added to the elite list of completing every Munro. I am in sympathy with such feelings and perhaps would have done likewise had I known about these non-conformists before my own completion. As it was, when I had completed the full round, I would not give in to my wife's wish to have my name added to the list. My climbing had been a very individual thing. Far from conquering the Munros, they had often conquered and humbled me, stripping away any swagger.

It is good to be humbled because with success the feat is even greater. We don't always achieve everything on our own and some things in life can be so intimidating that the expertise of another is welcome. It showed me how important it is to trust your guide. He had already earned that faith during the walk up to the ridge with his manner and testimony so that when the time came to trust his leading us safely up, he had already earned our confidence. A lesser man in those hostile conditions would have caused consternation. This climb struck me as a metaphor for the need to not only place our trust in God but also in those He puts around us to achieve the greater challenges of faith.

In doing something new I can be thankful that God has often provided a person to guide and to give confidence when taking those first steps. As a new Christian, a kindly vicar was my encourager as I started up a house group; or when helping to run a children's work for the first time, patient co-workers showed me the ropes. As a new missionary a very experienced Swiss woman gave much good advice in understanding tribal ways and to her we were much indebted. In each of the four tribal villages where we went on a regular basis, God again provided a local mentor from the people who came alongside to steer our way. One constant mentor, who continued through fifteen years of ministry, was David Manktelow, a semi-retired minister who wrote regularly, interacting with our prayer updates, who showed much evidence of prayerfully going with us. Out of this empathy, he often had a word that was just right to either make us think twice or to give the encouragement to go ahead. David was on the other side of the world from us and had never travelled or ministered in a tribal setting, but he had grown wise through the work God had given him and had learned how to encourage by God's word that he knew so well. He is an example of how to be highly effective although partially disabled through ill health. Frustrated by no longer being able to do the things he used to do as a church leader, David considered what the Lord would have him do now – and was taken in a direction which blessed us considerably.

MEDITATION

'Placing your Trust'

Some challenges in life really do require the help of another. Climbing the 'Inaccessible Pinnacle' was one of those challenges.

The awesome images seen on the In Pinn inspired a heady mixture of wonder and fear, confronting me with thoughts about the glory of the Lord:

O Lord my God, you are very great;
You are clothed with splendour and majesty.

He wraps himself in light as with a garment
... he makes the clouds his chariot
And rides on the wings of the wind.
He makes winds his messengers,
Flames of fire his servants.　　(Ps. 104:1-4)

Use this psalm and others like Psalms 96 and 97 to praise God. Use some of the terminology found in such psalms to enrich your vocabulary as well as the concept of praise.

Could you benefit from the mentoring of another, someone well experienced in the area you need help with? Consider whose advice/counsel could help you to achieve your aim? Could you shadow someone's ministry so that you can learn and gain understanding? The important ingredient is trust – you need to respect and feel confident in the other person's ability if you're really to be helped.

Do you have the vision to mentor another? This is especially purposeful if you're no longer able to do the work but can pass the encouragement and advice on to a younger person who may be taking up a ministry challenge or making a major life decision.

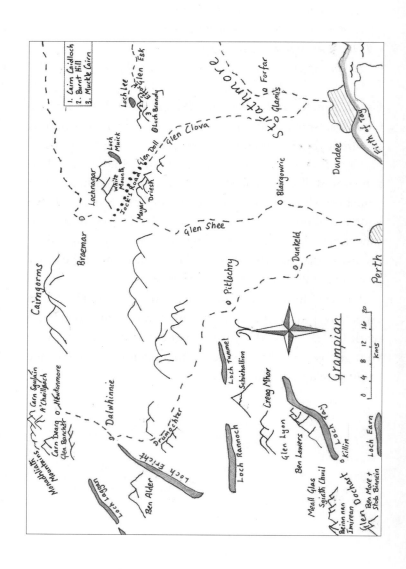

Cairn Caidloch
Burnt Hill
Muckle Cairn

Strathmore

Loch Lee
Glen Esk
Loch Brandy

Glen Clova
Glen Doll
Loch Muick
Lochnagar
White Mounth
Jock's Road
Mayar
Driesh

Glen Dell

Forfar
o Glamis

Dundee

Braemar

o Blairgowrie

Glen Shee

o Dunkeld

Firth of Tay

Cairngorms

o Pitlochry

Perth

Cairn Gulain
A'Chaillleach
o Newtonmore
Monadhliath
Cairn Dearg
Glen Banchor
Loch Laggan
Ben Alder
Loch Ericht

o Dalwhinnie
Drumochter

Loch Tummel
Schiehallion

Creag Mhor

Glen Lyon

Ben Lawers

Loch Rannoch

Loch Tay

Grampian

o Killin

Loch Earn

Meall Glas
Sgiath Chuil

Beinn nan
Imirean
Ben More +
Stob Binnein
Glen Dochart

0 4 8 12 16 20
kms

13

Moving Beyond Doubt

Glen Dochart and Monadh Liath

IN late March of 1991 I was already making my third hill outing of the year, reckoning an era was coming to a close, as we explored the possible calling to serve overseas that could take us from Scotland. Things were far from settled in our heads and even our hearts were ambivalent. The first half of that year I climbed more Munros than in any other six-month period, such was my concern at possibly not being able to climb for a while. Nothing was certain and the insecurity of our plans inspired a flurry of outings before a potential lengthy separation.

I intended climbing two Munros that overcast March day – Meall Glas and Sgiath Chuil – rising to the north of Glen Dochart (see 'Grampian' map, p. 134), where four years previously we had almost bought a large cottage to convert into a guesthouse. The deciding factor for not going ahead was its remote location and my wife's first pregnancy!

Hearing the call

The two craggy peaks are sighted from the road, separated by a pass dropping 1,000 feet beneath their summits. A private road provided a bridge access over the River Dochart but the way terminated at some buildings within 300 metres from the bridge. This was rather like the progress we had so far made in determining the way God was leading. The call seemed clear, bridging that major dividing line between a settled existence down on the floor of a sheltered glen, to living by faith up on the wild, wind-swept height. As we reviewed our possible future, the way looked very much like it did there at the foot of Meall Glas, a sure track that abruptly petered out into a rough moorland wilderness without path.

Our sense of calling was multifaceted. Firstly, there was the clear instruction from Jesus' parting words to His disciples, reminding them that all power and authority were His, won through the cross and evidenced by the resurrection from the dead and promise of eternal life. In view of this power and authority, Jesus tells His followers to take confidence and strength and to, 'Go and make disciples of all nations' (Matt. 28:19), offering a message of salvation, liberation and hope.

Secondly, we recognised our ease in relating to foreigners; enjoying their friendship, keen to understand and to respect their way of thinking and doing things. We had both worked for several years abroad, had learned other languages and continued to enjoy using these when receiving French and Italians in the guesthouse.

Thirdly, we were challenged by the example of a couple in our church who, with a young son, left Pitlochry to be part of a mission in Brazil. Somehow we had excused ourselves from leaving at this time in our lives because we had the responsibility of raising our children and that emigrating as a young family was just too big an upheaval.

Finally, we had the encouragement of other Christians whom we respected. Our good friends, Iain and Anne Cameron, who stayed across the River Tay from where we were in Birnam, ran a prayer group for the mission organisation OMF, which we became a part of. Other Christians from church, and missionaries who came to stay in our guesthouse, asked whether we wouldn't consider joining an international mission.

All of this seemed like a fine bridge helping us to cross the divide and when we focused just on that, everything seemed clear and in place.

The trek up Meall Glas felt a lonesome way requiring much effort to push on through the heather and tussocky grass without the encouragement of a path. The craggy goal was clear, but the climb was so arduous that I had to constantly resist giving up.

To respond to this mission call meant selling our business, giving up control of our own affairs, and to prepare at a Bible College for an unclear destination. For someone who enjoyed managing his own affairs it felt uncomfortable placing myself under the authority and direction of others. The relinquishing of independence was significant for me – I had really enjoyed being self-employed, of running a business in an ethical manner without having to make uncomfortable compromises, of building up such a successful enterprise that there was the need to move to bigger premises. This had prompted our putting the business up for sale and with this came the challenge of where was the Lord in all our planning?

> *Many are the plans in a man's heart,*
> *But it is the Lord's purpose that prevails.*   (Prov. 19:21)

If we were to contemplate change, then should we not be open to going overseas? At times this was an unwelcome question, an intrusion on how we would have liked to see things being worked out with us in total control. Just when we came to the conclusion that surrendering wasn't for us, we would be struck afresh in our Bible reading by such reminders:

> *Set your minds on things above not on earthly things.*
> (Col. 3:2)

I reached the col between Meall Glas and its outlying neighbour – Beinn nan Imirean – after a long, boggy slog over ground cover that was difficult and tediously slow to negotiate. It was a relief to reach this point, to have ground that was dry and firm underfoot at the watershed with a clear ridge line of short grass and gravel to follow. Twenty years later I pitched camp on this very col one fine May evening, watching the sunset framed in the open entrance of the tent. I was walking from St Andrews bound for Iona and this was a fine upland section not far from the halfway mark. The contrast was beautiful between the spring-green glen and the still winter aspect of Ben More and its twin of Stob Binnein. I had walked from Killin in the morning, following a hidden upland track halfway up in the hills.

Glen Dochart had a flimsy film of haze out of which twin gargantuan peaks, one conical and the other like a severed cone, both capped with snow, rose impressively, seeming higher than in reality. Years on I can still visualise the scene.

The best moments in fine weather camping are the unhurried evening hours. Passed, without the distraction of telephone or television, watching the deepening colours of the sunset, seeing the light grow dim and descend into that dark sapphire dusk when the first stars usher in the night. The impressions of the day's walking replay on the mind's eye, along with reflections made that day and thoughts of the way ahead. Thoughts of this climb of Meall Glas and the neighbouring Munro twenty years previously came to mind now along with all the troubled thoughts about our future.

The traverse of those two Munros brought some relief as I accepted things bigger than me. Up there on the high crags the world of men in the glens of Dochart and Lednock looked decidedly miniscule and unimportant below. My own plans to buy a small hotel seemed unimportant, an unworthy aim, and the Lord's calling to serve Him became more significant. As for our misgivings, I just had to trust the Lord. He knew my mind and my character and would be there for me as I worked through the challenges.

Clear marching orders

Two weeks later I was doing a round of three Munro summits in the Monadh Liath Hills just above Newtonmore (see also the 'Grampian' map, p. 134). We had had a couple of buyers who tendered their bids for our business that week. Our solicitor had called in the morning to let us know that he would call again after midday once the bids had been opened. During some anxious minutes of waiting, Iain, our son not yet four years old, had picked up on the nervousness. We will never forget him going into the corner of the room where our guitar was kept and bringing this across to me saying, 'Daddy, let's praise God!' As we sang, our own insecurities diminished as we focused on the One who controlled events. The phone rang as we were praising, informing us that an offer £30,000 in excess of our asking price had been made at a time the housing market was going through a slump. We heard our clear marching orders.

The walk from Newtonmore followed the big decision. In eight weeks we would be packing up. We felt relief that the indecision had passed, along with the tension of the unknown that brings with it swinging emotions. However, the apprehensions remained of what had we committed ourselves to? From Glen Banchor, I climbed a subsidiary glen rising to Loch Dubh, a fine ascent to a closing rim of steep-sided hills capped with imposing corries. I paused at Loch Dubh, the 'black loch', which had taken on a dark aspect beneath a sky of gathering storm clouds. I knew the Lord to be behind our calling to leave Scotland and that He would give us grace and understanding in helping us to overcome and to adapt through the many changes ahead. The thing that most concerned us was the probability we would be sending our two children to boarding school at some point.

I had been at a boarding school myself and had vowed I would never send my children away to school as my own experience had been so harrowing. Now the implications of mission life, if we were to go to South East Asia, would entail exactly that. My mood didn't get any easier as I sat contemplating the disturbed waters of the loch, the cold air from the hills dropping and pressing down upon the water, sent troubled patterns unpredictably across the surface. When I had shared these concerns with Gus Noble, the then director of OMF's Philippine field, who was staying at our guesthouse around this time, I well recall his empathy and his prayer when he quoted Psalm 126: 5-6. He spoke the words for us and indeed they proved true in the course of time:

Those who sow in tears
Will reap with songs of joy.
He who goes out weeping,
Carrying seed to sow,
Will return with songs of joy,
Carrying sheaves with him.

Feeling cold and increasingly morose, I pushed on for the first summit – Carn Dearg. A steep and persistent onslaught was required to make the summit. Although called the 'Red Hill', it was all white this day under fresh snow. The dark sky that I had noted down at Loch Dubh was now unleashing a fresh fall of snow that gained pace from hearty flurries to a full-blown blizzard. I pushed on along the eight kilometres of ridge walking that lay ahead, a high level way that rarely dropped beneath 3,000 feet leading to the next Munro. The snow gained depth surprisingly fast so that by the time I was halfway along this ridge, the going was decidedly tough, especially in the hollows and dips of the land where the snow had drifted. Losing time, I knew I had to push even harder if I were to complete the tour of the three summits before nightfall. Carn Sgulain was finally reached after three hours rather than the estimated two, and I was feeling very tired. A change of bearing from Carn Sgulain, worked in my favour, now directing me towards the car beyond the third Munro. Thankfully, the snow cover seemed easier as I descended to the col and then climbed the last Munro of the day named A' Chailleach – 'the old woman' or 'hag' – an earth-goddess figure our ancient Pict forebears were in fear of and who needed to be placated with votive offerings.

Keep the task in sight

The outing had been particularly strenuous, steeling me for our future. Hillcraft had taught me much about the need to prepare, which we were about to do at Moorlands Bible College. I also learnt to keep the task in sight, of living out a Christian witness wherever we went. What had impacted me was the need to push on prayerfully and to persevere when opposition arose.

> *Endure hardship with us like a good soldier of Christ Jesus. No-one serving as a soldier gets involved in civilian affairs – he wants to please his commanding officer.*
> (2 Tim. 2:3-4)

I cannot say that I looked ahead with a carefree attitude once our decision was made. I saw a task far bigger than I could handle alone; I knew we required heavenly resources if we were to succeed. But we had an inner conviction that drove us, and together with an intellectual agreement based on an understanding of scripture, this brought approval to the task. All circumstances suggested we were being prepared for this assignment.

We faced significant opposition from parents, somewhat understandably, as they didn't share our faith. We were surprised at how extreme this attack could be from those who loved us, but they were obviously hurting. As a consequence it made us go out of our way to keep in touch when overseas, so they would see all the developments of their grandchildren. We took considerable care to regularly write and to send family video films to them. When we returned on our first leave four years later, a great change had taken place in their attitudes. We saw them move from being embittered to being proud of what we were doing.

The power of the Lord

And the change of attitude wasn't just with our parents, but in ourselves too. By the time we had worked with the Buhid tribe on Mindoro in the Philippines for seven years, we had seen the power of the Lord in setting people free from fears of the demonic. We had seen His grace and commitment in taking some unlikely people and transforming them into inspiring leaders. We too could testify to God's gentle grace in His commitment to us. Although encountering difficult times – not least the separation from children – God enabled us to bear with these things and gave us a vision of Himself that we would never have had, had we stayed in Scotland. I can never doubt God and His existence, for His works are clear to see. But the joyful, spiritual breakthroughs that swept through these tribal communities, the release from extreme spiritual oppression, the contentment of being in Christ despite being at the very bottom of the pecking order and being discriminated against – all of this made God so real that to this day I cannot doubt.

What became more difficult upon our return to Scotland was sensing a lack of joy that people took in following Jesus.

The tribal people we lived with in the Philippines counted it as such a joy to be in Christ. Christ was their everything, their 'very great reward'. They quite literally longed to be with Him in a heaven where the huge injustices they faced day by day would no longer happen. This helped them endure their daily lot, such as keeping their hope in Christ in their great poverty; coping prayerfully with illness with little or no resource to medicine or health care, and the injustices caused by aggressive outsiders snatching their land or carrying out acts of sabotage. They weren't perfect and they had their less enthusiastic moments but when they were centred on Christ there was something extremely winsome about their fervent faith that I have rarely encountered back in the West. We were shown a faith that stood up under great tests, providing an example that continues to help us consider our own trials that are often trivial inconveniences in comparison to theirs. We've learnt to treat *trivial inconveniences* as such and to quickly overcome them. We hope that the bigger trials that we've faced, such as my wife's battle with cancer, have been faced with a measure of the faith and fortitude that our tribal family demonstrated. These were lessons that we had to learn on the other side of the world, far from home, but they were lessons we were glad to have under God's guidance.

MEDITATION

'Moving beyond Doubt'

We sometimes shirk the call of God because we're comfortable with the status quo in our lives. The challenge seems such an upheaval, too great to undertake, beyond our experience and expertise. But that is often where God would lead us so that we may be more dependent upon Him through prayer and Bible study.

Sometimes it's not unwillingness or disobedience that makes us timid but sheer doubt in our ability to achieve what God is calling us to do. The doubt is so much that we question that we have heard correctly.

Does this describe the place where you are at? Is there a conflict in the advice you're getting? Does this call have a scriptural base? Re-examine the scriptures prayerfully, taking note of the context and situation in which these are set to understand what originally is being conveyed. Are you still feeling the urge of the Spirit to examine your own life and future in the light of what these scriptures are saying? Are these backed up by the counsel of mature Christians you respect?

Is your reluctance based on fear? Does there appear to be a loss factor – a loss of independence that it's no longer you who's responsible for making life choices? This can all seem too much.

I recall reading these words on a notice placed on a bed-side table and thinking how simply and aptly they are stated:

The will of God will never take you,
Where the grace of God cannot keep you.

From the poem *The Will of God* – author unknown.

This is reassuring. Consider times in your life when this truth has been known. Allow this to build up faith for whatever challenge is maybe before you. Often the joy of a spiritual connection with God as a result of following Him helps us again to move beyond doubt.

God seeks to bless us and to make us a blessing to others (the form of Abraham's call in Genesis 12:2-3). He asks us to move forward confidently in the victory and supremacy that has been demonstrated by the cross and the resurrection. Matthew 28:18-20 assures us that we're not going it alone, but His special presence is there.

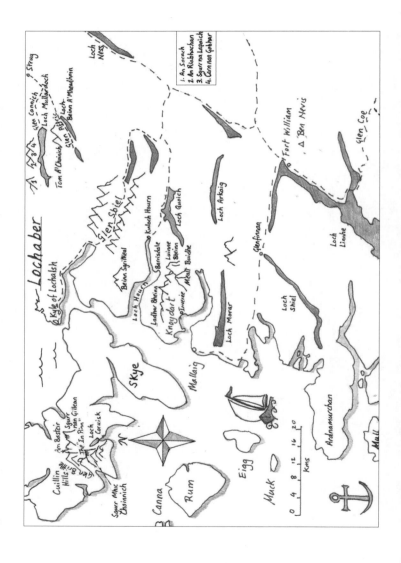

Loch Ness

9 Stray
Glen Cannich
Loch Mullardoch
Loch
Glen Affric
Beinn A'Mheadhoin

1. An Socach
2. An Riabhachan
3. Sgurr na Lapaich
4. Carn nan Gobhar

Tom A'Choinich

Fort William

△ Ben Nevis

Glen Coe

Lochaber

Glen Shiel

Loch Arkaig

Loch Quoich

Kyle of Lochalsh

Beinn Sgritheal

Kinloch Hourn

Benisdale
Luinne Bheinn
Meall Buidhe

Glenfinnan

Loch Linnhe

Loch Hourn

Ladhar Bheinn
Knoydart
Inverie

Loch Shiel

Skye

Mallaig

Loch Morar

An Bastier
Sgurr nan Gillean
Sgurr
"The In Pinn"
Loch Coruisk

Cuillin Hills

Sgurr Mhic Choinnich

Canna

Rum

Eigg

Muck

0 4 8 12 16 20
Kms

Ardnamurchan

Mull

148

14

Adoration Greater Than Vision

Glen Affric Hills

FIVE years after climbing Meall Glas and the hills described in the previous chapter we had returned to Scotland for a year's home assignment, providing an opportunity again of hillwalking. One walk from Glen Affric (see 'Lochaber' map, p. 149) particularly stands out.

The splendour of the thickly wooded shoreline of Loch Beinn a' Mheadhoin entranced me as I set off to stretch stiff legs after the long car journey. The steady climb up a subsidiary glen to reach the two Munros was most easily accessed from Glen Affric but the peaks remained unsighted from the road. That evening I was due to speak at a prayer meeting in Inverness and not wanting to be pushed for time I had made an early start on the hill at 6 a.m., not to just achieve the hill challenge, but to savour it and take time to be still, to contemplate what the future held as I prepared to return to the Philippines for another mission term.

The first three kilometres were done in great eagerness, encouraged in part by the race of the adjacent burn. The pace would not have mattered had I been fitter, but as I emerged from a forest on completing the first stage I was suddenly humbled by sighting the major climb yet ahead. The snow-capped peak of Tom a' Choinich intermittently came in and out of view as clouds gathered, dispersing only to then quickly reform. The peak's darkly brooding flanks had substantial sheets of snow on that checked my formerly confident pace.

I thought ahead to our imminent return to the Philippines and wondered what this next mission term had in store. There was the challenge of inspiring the churches to be more outward looking, to consider their neighbours – the Bangon sub-tribe – in the less accessible hills. A tribe that had been traumatised by the spirit world in which they lived. I wondered how this was to be done and as I did so an outline of a strategy began to form in my mind.

The approach to Tom a' Chonich doesn't look difficult on a map, a mere seven centimetres across the flat paper surface make it look so do-able. I'm sure that someone fit would breeze up and back in a morning! But I wasn't that man and unknown to me at that time, I was struggling with the gathering progression of tuberculosis contracted towards the end of my first term in the Philippines.I would only learn about this condition a couple of months later when going through the quarantine procedures of the Philippine immigration process during our application for a resident visa.

Rainbow promise

With considerable moisture in the air, whenever the sun broke through the clouds rainbows formed and dissolved. Rainbows always bring me encouragement – a covenant sign of promise that God will do what He says. Sighting these rainbows emerging and re-forming as I walked the trail up the narrow glen gave me renewed vigour. I continued to think about how best to reach the remote subgroup of the tribe that had adopted us realising that how to accomplish this was becoming a neat summary in my head.

Focus on the Lord

A rainbow shone brilliantly for a moment and then dissolved as storm clouds blew overhead sending a dark foreboding aspect over the ben ahead. Suddenly I was struck by my pre-occupation with my work rather than what should have been adoration of the One who would make it all possible. The rainbow reminded me of heavenly blessing, without which nothing of any eternal worth would endure. The dark aspect of the mountain also brought to mind the otherworldliness of the Lord and that He wasn't someone just to be won over to do our bidding, someone standing on the touchlines awaiting our intervention. I was checked in my tracks that my focus on plans had taken my eyes away from the Lord. However worthy my goals were, seeking the Lord was the ultimate focus.

Moses' encounter with the burning bush came to mind. God had on His agenda the rescue of His people from their slavery in Egypt by sending Moses, a former prince who had for the past forty years become a nobody of a shepherd in the wilderness, to be the rescuer of the Israelites. The starting point, his commissioning as it were, was the encounter with the Lord in the flaming bush that was not consumed. This moment brought with it a tremendous awe of God (Exodus 3:6). I too recognised the Lord's splendour. From that point on in my climb, He became my focus, my prayer was a thirsting to know more of Him.

In time, again I felt lethargic, my boots heavy with mud and moisture I stumbled amongst the heather and along a stony way. The ben was lost from view and a snowy cold bore down upon me slowing my movements. What had started out as a very pleasant trip rising steadily from the beauty of the wooded loch took on the nature of an ordeal and I wasn't sure whether it felt good anymore to be on the hill. As if on cue, the sun burst through from the east and wreathed me for a brief moment in its embracing light. As I was heading westward, the sun behind cast a bold shadow before me, like an ethereal companion urging me on and I took this metaphorically that the Lord was with me, an encouragement that didn't diminish as the light was shrouded once again and the wintry weather closed in with steely sleet blasting my face with frosty talons.

Every tribe

I had a presentiment that the next term in the Philippines was going to be contested, that there would be agonies, delays and deaths, and yet I also had a great assurance that God would be with me, that His purposes would not be thwarted. His intention to rescue those from the sub-tribe was a completed task for the Lord of Time. Days do not confine the Lord, He doesn't need to fight against the tide of years like a mortal being. Neither is the Lord fixed at a point in time like us mortals. God has promised to gather some from that sub-tribe in; and there in the eternal scheme of things, where there is no yesterday, tomorrow or today, some from the Bangon, that sub-tribe, already stood in His protective presence. In the new song sung to the lamb in heaven, this chorus reminds us that there will be people from all nations in heaven:

You are worthy to take the scroll
and to open its seals,
because you were slain,
and with your blood you
purchased men for God
from every tribe and language and
people and nation.
You have made them to be a kingdom
And priests to serve our God,
And they will reign on the earth.   (Rev. 5:9-10)

The climb continued, its gradient challenging to a weakened body and the weather worsened as the ascent continued up the exposed ridge. The wind came unchecked, the altitude made the chill more apparent and although the summit was lost from sight, I was undeterred. I knew it to be there. The sun was shut out, but despite the dark ferocity of the storm clouds, it could not blank out altogether the proof of its existence. I didn't need to be some super champion, nor to sprint; I only had to plod, faithful step after weary step, knowing that eventually I would arrive at the summit, because its peak was fixed and I was on course. Encouraged by the illuminating thoughts of God's presence and eternal plans I had strength that was from within and nothing, no power would frustrate God's purposes. I only had to hold fast to the knowledge of His presence and His promise. I found shelter on the climb behind a rock. A comfort, instilling fresh strength.

Of course I could have just stopped and turned back, given up. To do successful hillwalking requires setting your face to the summit and pursuing this goal. God gave me that breather in the shelter of a rock, breaking the task into stages. Every step was progress, one less stage to do, the ground already covered an encouragement that the threat of the toil ahead diminished. Then the summit was attained. That one time distant point that made you question whether it could be reached was there at my feet.

The one who watches over me

Well that was the first summit of the day, not reached easily, and yet another summit remained across vast tracts of peat morass. The peaty ground felt symbolic of human despair, where progress can be so disheartening with its slip and slide taking up so much energy for the small progress forward. Craggy outcrops emerged out of the mist, but the map had warned of their presence, and I knew to expect the dread of opposition from forces that were intimidating whilst at the same time knowing who my keeper is. The One who watches over me and strengthens the arm of His servants.

> *He reached down from on high and took hold of me;*
> *He drew me out of deep waters.*
> *He rescued me from the strong enemy,*
> *From my foes, who were too strong for me.*
> *They confronted me in the day of disaster,*
> *But the Lord was my support,*
> *He brought me out into a spacious place;*
> *He rescued me because he delighted in me.*
>   (Ps. 18:16-19)

In the mist the depths looked greater, and spectral-like they haunted the way for a while, seeking to discourage, which they did when given undue attention, symbolic of the things that seem fearful and upsetting. It was crucial to be aware of the sure presence of the Lord, He had enabled the progress so far and half the journey was already completed. If He could bring me there, why would He not lead me through to the journey's end?

And to the final stage He did lead me. The long but gradual descent from the heights began, the ferocity of the wind abated and the sun's rays broke through the storm clouds. The sun traced the homeward way, lighting up the silver thread of the burn, leading all the way to the glittering jewels dancing on the surface of the loch at journey's end. This day's walk often came to mind as a kind of allegory whilst events over the following three years in the Philippines unfolded.

MEDITATION

'Adoration Greater than Vision'

'Adoration greater than vision' is a challenge to where our focus is applied. Have the goals of a Christian task exceeded our experience and worship of God? In the Glen Affric hills I faced this challenge and had to confess that the task had become more consuming than my pursuit of the Lord. The walk was allegorical of the challenges facing us in our next missionary term and proved to be a timely corrective to focus on the greatness of the Lord rather than my energy and vision to work out the strategy to fulfil the task.

Do you tend to get ahead of yourself and ahead of the Lord, of neatly mapping out how a task is going to be achieved? Are you guilty of thinking it's all about your preparation: the course syllabus of your Bible teaching, your credentials, your training, your degree? Is it all achievable because the vision is rubber-stamped by the elders/deacons and has funds from the treasurer? Are you guilty of what one missionary bravely admitted, that others had better pray for breakthroughs as he was too busy doing the work?

This is stark – too busy to pray. If that's you, stop in your tracks and acknowledge the folly of ministry without prayer; of planning without seeking God's counsel; of frantic commotion without God's direction. One of the so-called 'Servant Songs' in Isaiah indicates the type of servant God will use to lead His people back to trust and worship:

> *The Sovereign Lord has given me an instructed tongue,*
> *To know the word that sustains the weary.*
> *He wakens me morning by morning,*
> *Wakens my ear to listen like one being taught.*
> *The Sovereign Lord has opened my ears,*
> *And I have not been rebellious;*
> *I have not drawn back.*   (Isa. 50:4-5)

Note the attitude of waiting and listening first so that we may be instructed in what to say and what to do. Because of the servant's love for and dependence upon God, the servant rises early as well as consistently to have undisturbed time to relate to God. Why? In order to have something of consequence to say to 'sustain the weary'. When we bring the concerns of our lives, our loved ones and all those God has placed around us into the quiet place, God can direct by giving us a burden for someone and often along with that the clarity of what we should say or do. This kind of ministry is more fruitful when it is an outcome of prayer, of sensing the Lord's will and directive, than all the many good works we think we should be doing.

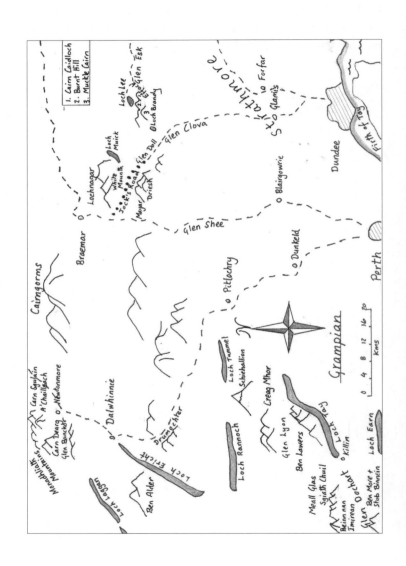

1. Cairn Caidloch
2. Burnt Hill
3. Muckle Cairn

Cairngorms

Braemar

Glen Shee

Glen Clova

Glen Doll

Glen Esk

Loch Lee

Loch Brandy

Loch Muick

White Mouth

Jock's Road

Mayar

Driesh

Lochnagar

Stathmore

to Forfar

Glamis

Blairgowrie

Dundee

Dunkeld

Pitlochry

Perth

Firth of Tay

Grampian

kms

0 4 8 12 16 20

Loch Tummel

Schiehallion

Creag Mhor

Glen Lyon

Ben Lawers

Loch Tay

Killin

Loch Earn

Loch Rannoch

Meall Glas

Sgiath Chuil

Ben More +

Stob Binnein

Glen Dochart

Beinn nan

Imirean

Loch Laggan

Ben Alder

Loch Ericht

Dalwhinnie

Drumochter

Monadhliath

Carn Dearg

Glen Banchor

Newtonmore

Cairn Sgulain

A'Chaillpach

15

In Adversity

Ben Wyvis and the Stobs of the Black Mount

CONFRONTING a crippling torpor, I was driving north over the Drumochter Pass (see 'Grampian' map, p. 158) on a clear December night bound for Ben Wyvis (see 'Wester Ross' map, p. 80). With little traffic, I slowed, wound down the window to breathe in the damp, earthy smell of the hills and to trace their dark outlines under starry skies. Three and a half years had passed without a hill climb, marking the time of being abroad in the Philippines, and I was already anticipating the excitement of returning to the Munros. Six months earlier I had returned to Scotland broken in health, recovering from the lingering aftermath of Dengue fever and still regaining stamina after overcoming TB two years earlier. It was time to try a hill again after months of inactivity and the frustration of taking to my bed in the middle of the day totally washed out. I took the secondary road through the Rothiemurchus Forest just to enjoy the fine silhouettes of the ancient Caledonian pines. The moon rose huge and magnificent that night, full-orbed, sweeping the snow-topped Cairngorms with penetrating light. I was finally back home in the Northlands, to an environment where I felt I most belonged and to a creation that so inspired and soothed. The solace it brought my weary soul was immeasurable.

The following day, Ben Wyvis, perhaps meaning 'hill of terror', presented something of that face to me, proving to be an arduous climb for someone neither fit nor back to full health. But I pressed on by way of homage to the old familiar way, delighting in the invigorating tug of the December wind and the stunning chill of that altitude. The year's moorland grass, dried and bleached a straw colour, still looked sprightly blowing lustily in the wind that combed the hillsides. The morning sun rose slowly with rays of deep ochre and held a day-long benediction upon my forehead from its low winter's zenith. I felt revived, returning to the very essence of the Highlands, back to this lovely pastime I had so missed. It might have been seen as a bit foolhardy tackling the ben in my condition and in the grip of winter chill, but then I argued it was a simple matter of a relatively short out and back excursion, the outward section the more demanding being the ascent. I reasoned that if I were to cut my losses part way through this would only entail an easy descent back to the car. The inner urge to walk was all compelling and the Lord strengthened me that day to reach the summit and helped me turn a significant corner towards a fuller recovery.

A season of weariness and frustration continued, though this slowly diminished. Five months later, having regained strength and healed from the illness that dogged me in the tropics, my family and I decided we were all ready to return to the Philippines only for those hopes to be dashed within a week or two by some who thought otherwise. Their advice: this was a time to remain and put down roots for a time.

Totally unexpected, this dealt a crushing blow leaving us without any plan of what to do next. We had been so focused on returning that we hadn't even thought what else we could do. We felt devastated, like victims caught up in an accident, having to respond to new circumstances. In the first shockwave of this bad news we couldn't get beyond our feelings of dismay, seeing the flaws in the reasoning of others that kept us back. I remember the sense of outrage vividly and I find it helpful to recall so I can show how we processed this great disappointment.

Dismayed with God

Next came the dismay with God – why had He permitted this to happen when we saw clearly that we were needed in our roles overseas? Events just didn't square with our belief in God's calling. There followed much well-meant sympathy, as others identified with our new situation and expressed dismay. The wishes of colleagues in the Philippines and those with whom we worked was that somehow we would be able to return in a little while. All of this amounted to a considerable sum of reasons to feel very sorry for ourselves. We felt stupefied.

The initial thing that helped us gain a more godly perspective was to recognise that what had happened wasn't merely the flawed arbitrations of man, but that God had permitted this as part of His sovereign will. I find Job's observations as he processes the disasters that had come upon him particularly helpful.

> *His (the Lord's) wisdom is profound, his power is vast.*
> *Who has resisted him and come out unscathed?*
> *He moves mountains without their knowing it*
> *And overturns them in his anger.*
> *He shakes the earth from its place and makes its pillars tremble.*
> *He speaks to the sun and it does not shine;*
> *He seals off the light of the stars.*
> *He alone stretches out the heavens and treads on the waves of the sea.*
> *He is the Maker of the Bear and the Orion,*
> *The Pleiades and the constellations of the south.*
> *He performs wonders that cannot be fathomed,*
> *Miracles that cannot be counted.*
> *When he passes me, I cannot see him;*
> *When he goes by, I cannot perceive him.*
> *If he snatches away, who can stop him?*
> *Who can say to him 'What are you doing?'* (Job 9:4-12)

This first step of identifying God's sovereignty isn't easy to take. In our human rationale, and as part of the age in which we live, we look for causes, build up our arguments, apportion blame and pronounce a party as being responsible and therefore guilty. We get stuck in a rut when we see things purely on a human level and lose our peace until we reason with God under the firm assumption that nothing happens outside of His will.

*And we know that in all things God works for the good
of those who love him, who have been called according
to his purpose.* (Rom. 8:28)

Often the manner in which events unfold can show much
human fault, so much so, that we find it hard to accept that
God has permitted it. This is what Job suggests about God
in the lines:

*When he passes me, I cannot see him;
When he goes by, I cannot perceive him.* (Job 9:11)

It's all right to air our grievances to God. Our prayers should
be honest just as some of the Psalms are very earthy in trying
to make sense of circumstances. This openness and honesty
with God is part of the process of coming to terms with the
situation. It is better to have a rant with God directly in
prayer than to rant about God to others.

As westerners we don't find the oriental fatalism expressed
by Job as something easy to accept; the acceptance that
difficulties are sometimes dealt by God along with the
creature response of 'Who are we to question?'. We like to
think of ourselves as masters of events and circumstances,
an attitude which scientific progress has compounded. We
shouldn't accept things as they are. Whilst this is positive in
the fight against cancer and HIV for example, it becomes
a negative when we want to address difficult circumstances
only to discover it's beyond our power. This leads to a sense
that we have the right to demand of God, "What are you
doing?" For as long as we lock horns with the Almighty, we
are in a state of utter stalemate and can even shipwreck our

faith on account of it. It might seem unsatisfactory to our modern minds to state the fundamental truth that God is God and that He can do as He likes; but that is the crux of the matter. God doesn't have to account for Himself.

The Lord gave and the Lord has taken away

Even Job with these flashes of fatalistic acceptance isn't able to maintain his composure for long, protesting that he has been unjustly treated. On the premise that Job has got his just desserts for some undisclosed sin that his friends are insistent he has committed, Job rigorously protests his innocence. The friends' argument that bad things happen on account of wrongdoing is flawed thinking. Bad things happen to the innocent too, as in Job's case as we shall see.

The book of Job concludes with God's response:

Who is this that darkens my counsel with words
*   without knowledge?*
Brace yourself like a man; I will question you and you
*   shall answer me.*   (Job 38:2-3)

Will the one who contends with the Almighty correct him?
Let him who accuses God answer him!   (Job 40:2)

In other words, who are we to question the actions of God? Our understanding is far too finite, as God illustrates by saying that man doesn't have an explanation for how God orchestrated each step of the creation; so if we cannot fathom these basics, then who are we to question the purposes of His will when the innocent suffer? On one level, we find the reason why God permits suffering unsatisfactory, why should all these things have happened to Job? However, we as the reader have the benefit of being assured of his innocence for at the opening of the book Job is declared to be 'blameless and upright; he feared God and shunned evil' (1:1). This is the contention that Job wrestles with throughout. What Job doesn't know is that there is a heavenly battle taking place. Satan states that Job only worships God because God has blessed him. Remove the blessings, Satan declares, strike at his wealth and family, then Job will curse God. God allows this to happen as it's a part of His will and Job unexpectedly responds with, 'The Lord gave and the Lord has taken away; may the name of the Lord be praised' (Job 1:21).

Satan then raises the stakes by saying to the Lord, 'Stretch out your hand and strike his flesh and bones, and he will surely curse you to your face' (Job 2:5). Job maintains sufficient integrity, although he wonders and rants and protests, suffering much throughout. We can identify easily with the protests. But we need to move beyond the bellyaching if we are to progress any further in a constructive way and move beyond self-pity.

It takes Job the whole of the forty-two chapter book to come to recognise that he, a finite being with very limited knowledge, has no right to question God once he considers the immeasurable immensity of God's being, creativity and eternal purposes, 'Surely I spoke of things I did not understand, things too wonderful for me to know' (Job 42: 3). He senses that God will ultimately set all things to rights with the same assumption that Abraham used when he declared, 'Will not the Judge of all the earth do right?' (Gen. 18:25). Job has the premonition that

God will vindicate, that He the Judge will work salvation and will also become the Redeemer:

I know that my Redeemer lives,
And in the end he will stand upon the earth. (Job 19:25)

This is the spine-tingling prophetic glimpse ahead to Christ, of God entering our human condition to identify with us, experiencing suffering yet with saving power to free us from our protests and rebellion against God.

Blessed be the name of the Lord

We have observed a process that begins with dismay, ranting, arguing one's innocence, apportioning blame elsewhere and of feeling very sorry for yourself. Progress begins when we begin to bring all the trouble to God and this progress gains pace with the assertion that God is sovereign however messily it seems His will has been carried out. Airing our grievances to God is more helpful than ranting to others but this needs to ultimately recognise that we who are finite are not equal to question God's ways and are not here to argue the perceived injustices of His ruling. We see only in part and don't perceive the events being carried out in the heavenlies and therefore our understanding is limited. Trust is required in reckoning that God knows what He is doing and that ultimately He will do what is right – although that might not be within the context of our brief time on earth.

I needed to take to the hills to lay that disappointment before the Lord. I set out to climb the two 'Stobs' or 'peaks' – Stob a' Choire Odhair and Stob Ghabher (see 'Mull and Argyll' map, p. 102) – rising above Loch Tulla off the Glen

Coe road, still unfit, but stronger than when I had struggled up Ben Wyvis. A day of moody clouds intermittently unleashing their icy showers expressed my inner turmoil. But I had the bit between my teeth to combat an all-consuming self-pity. This blast in the hills was an intended antidote, praying as I walked that I would overcome, by appropriating the truths about God I had been pondering.

Not that this was a done and dusted matter with no further doubts and questions and protests. But when the protests came, I committed these to the Lord, asking Him to help me overcome this unproductive negativity and to bring me to a point of acceptance that this was His will and therefore I had no further contention with man. And I wasn't going to contend with God. I accepted that He knew what He was doing albeit remaining a mystery to me.

I recognised the need to move on, to stop asking the unanswerable 'Why?' question, to not get stuck in a rut re-playing the dialogues and all the time nursing the hurt. Instead I had to ask what was next. I found Paul's determination in overcoming past regrets most helpful in fashioning a steely resolve in me to do likewise:

> *I press on to take hold of that for which Christ Jesus took hold of me. Brothers, I do not consider myself yet to have taken hold of it. But one thing I do: Forgetting what is behind and straining towards what is ahead, I press on towards the goal to win the prize for which God has called me heavenwards in Christ Jesus.* (Phil. 3:12-14)

'Forgetting what is behind' was a great liberation for me, consigning the big regret and the mystery of it all to the past, which we can more effectively do by focusing our energies positively on 'straining towards what is ahead'. Great acceptance came when I acknowledged God was in control, that He and not man had closed the door and therefore this was an occasion for trust, to move forward in the belief that God had something new for us. That made all the difference and transformed my outlook. It required faith in the One who saw all and had planned it this way. This trust won me peace. But it had to be a proactive trust, to cease kicking against the goads and face it with all my will. Spiritual transformation is often the result of a battle of the will responding to heavenly guidance, choosing to move on from regret or defeat. It's not a one-time process, but a willful repetition of the same resolve, a taking 'captive every thought to make it obedient to Christ' (2 Cor. 10:5).

Somewhere between the two Munros, in the mist-filled basin, I sought instinctively for the route upwards, out of the bog, on to firmer ground. It came upon me there – as I struggled, sometimes on my hands up the steepness of the brae – to write about those years spent with a Filipino tribe who had adopted us. For the remainder of the walk, each step increased my enthusiasm for the book project, with many of the themes taking shape there and then with the sharp clarity of a sudden revelation which later developed further as I set about the task of writing. The project proved very cathartic and brought a sense of closure. With the benefit of hindsight, setting down what God had done with a tribe who came strongly under the influence of His word and Spirit, helped immeasurably to see that it was God's timing to withdraw us at the moment when the tribe had found renewed confidence in the ways of the Lord. Left to us, we might have outstayed our usefulness and delayed the coming of age of a church. The book was a thread of light during a very testing period (underscored by the telling statistic of not climbing any hills for the next two years), bringing me into a more intimate relationship with God at a time when human friendships were very sparse.

The plaintive comments in Psalm 102:6-7 echoed the loneliness I felt, but whilst these feelings were long-lasting, they did fade over the following three years and God proved faithful:

I am like a desert owl,
Like an owl among the ruins.
I lie awake; I have become
Like a bird alone on a roof.

Near the close of the Psalm comes the consolation:

But you remain the same,
And your years will never end.   (v. 27)

MEDITATION

'In Adversity'

How do we deal with a crushing disappointment that totally alters our life – a redundancy; contracting cancer; a failed marriage; a rebellious child that has abandoned the home; a personal disgrace?

Will we ever stop ranting to others? To rant for a little while is maybe understandable and tolerated but when it becomes habitual, we get nowhere and make ourselves so odious that others start to avoid us. We need to move quickly beyond blame, even though that's what our western culture dictates. Blame will make us embittered, prisoners to hatred, nurturing an unforgiving spirit that colours the whole complexion of life.

To rise above adversity starts in acknowledging that God, being absolutely sovereign, has permitted this to happen, however humanly messy it might appear to be. So it might be appropriate for you to protest to the Lord as we see in some very honest psalms. When our energy is spent, begin asking the Lord, 'Well, what now? What's next?' This is the beginning of moving beyond adversity. The experience will have humbled us, perhaps stripped us of confidence, maybe even brought us through a breakdown. Perhaps this is where God needed to lead us to make us dependent! It was like this for Nebuchadnezzar who was stripped of his reason for a time and lived with the wild animals. This pagan despot was brought to his senses and acknowledged God in the process of his suffering when he said:

His dominion is an eternal dominion;
His kingdom endures from generation to generation.
All the peoples of the earth are regarded as nothing.
He does as he pleases with the powers of heaven
and the peoples of the earth.
No-one can hold back his hand
or say to him: 'What have you done?' (Dan. 4:34-35)

It's also noteworthy that God didn't call Moses when he was prince of Egypt, but after he became a non-entity in the Midian desert minding sheep. Sometimes we need to be humbled in order to be surrendered to God.

Consider, is your disappointment pointing towards His appointment of you? What is God saying? Clear the distortion of your raving and take time out to be still enough to actually listen and heed.

I will exalt you, O Lord,
For you lifted me out of the depths
And did not let my enemies gloat over me.
O Lord my God, I called to you for help and you
*   healed me.*
O Lord, you brought me up from the grave;
You spared me from going down into the pit.
Sing to the Lord, you saints of his; praise his holy
*   name.*
For his anger lasts only a moment,
But his favour lasts a lifetime;
Weeping may remain for a night,
But rejoicing comes in the morning.   (Ps. 30:1-5)

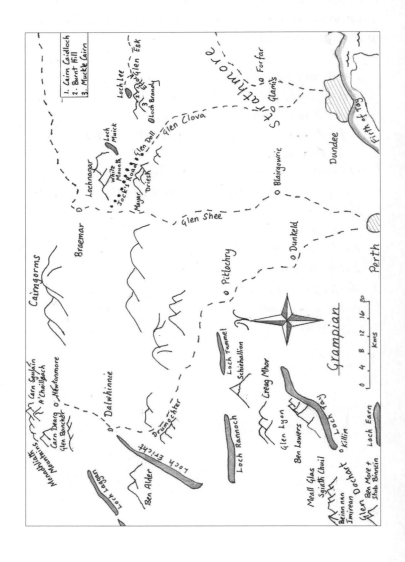

1. Cairn Caidloch
2. Burnt Hill
3. Muckle Cairn

Strathmore

to Forfar
Loch Lee
to Glamis
Glen Esk
Loch Brandy
Glen Clova
Loch Muick
Firth of Tay
Lochnagar
Glen Doll
White Mounth
Jock's Road
Dundee
Mayar
Driesh
Braemar
Blairgowrie
Cairngorms
Glen Shee
Dunkeld
Pitlochry
Perth
Carn Sgulain
A'Chailleach
Carn Dearg
Newtonmore
Monadhliath
Mountains
Glen Banchor
Dalwhinnie
Grampian
Loch Tummel
Schiehallion
Creag Mhor
Drumochter
0 4 8 12 16 20
kms
Ben Alder
Loch Ericht
Loch Laggan
Loch Rannoch
Glen Lyon
Loch Tay
Killin
Ben Lawers
Loch Earn
Meall Glas
Sgiath Chuil
Beinn nan
Imirean
Glen Dochart
Ben More
Stob Binnein

172

16

Walking by Faith and not by Sight

Drumochter Hills

I didn't set out to 'bag' Munros. I heard about a catalogue of the heights only after climbing twenty-two of them. I would have been made aware of this elite classification earlier had I been part of a hillwalking club, or climbed with other enthusiasts. Ironically, it was Alexandra who drew them to my attention by gifting me a Munro book on my birthday back in 1988. She might have regretted the present since it made her life lonelier, as I felt the call to the hills all the more. However, she did remark that I was more likeable after a blast in the hills.

'How long did they take you?' is the question often posed by those who know you have completed the whole round. Most people are dimly aware that there are quite a few and it's something of a feat requiring commitment and perseverance to have done the full tour. Most are surprised that there are as many as 282 distinct summits of over 3,000 feet (according to the last survey and confirmed by the Scottish Mountaineering Club in September 2012, although no doubt this total will be adjusted again with possible new contenders for Munro status and others to be demoted). More surprisingly still in my case is that they took all of forty years to complete. This length was partly due to being brought up in England and then later spending fourteen years living overseas, making for a slow tally, especially when so many outings ascend only one or just two Munros. Even when living in Scotland, outings needed to be spaced out so as to enjoy family life and share in its responsibilities. Outings during the summer in the guesthouse were impossible as being tied by the demands of high season made a brief trip to the rubbish tip or to the shops a treat just to escape from being housebound. As noted earlier I was also very wary of venturing into the hills on my own in the winter. In a good year I would only make about twelve sorties and at times climbing all 282 summits seemed unattainable before becoming old and decrepit, affecting my focus and motivation.

To hear the Lord speaking into your life

Focused determination is required to apply yourself regularly to fulfil an ongoing challenge, to avoid being swamped by the everyday activities of life. It sometimes takes creativity, and most definitely intentionality, to seek opportunities to make outings happen, fixing an appointment in the diary with the hills. How many of us fall into the rut, give up on realising dreams feeling they're beyond reach? How easy to allow life's circumstances to overwhelm intent. For me these hill outings are mostly about creating time to engage with God. For you to hear the Lord speaking into your life it may take a commitment to participate in a guided retreat or to take part in a church away weekend if you find interaction with others essential.

There is a good deal about determination and focus spoken of in the New Testament and here are just a couple of the better known examples:

Let us throw off everything that hinders and the sin that so easily entangles, and let us run with perseverance the race marked out for us. Let us fix our eyes upon Jesus, the author and perfecter of our faith, who for the joy set before him endured the cross, scorning its shame … Consider him who endured such opposition from sinful men, so that you will not grow weary and lose heart. (Heb. 12:1-3)

Like doing the round of Munros, the Christian life isn't just a sprint here and there, although the sprints are good for coming up to speed again and getting back on track after a time of slowly dragging our feet. Discipleship is about focused commitment, of keeping heaven always upon the horizon so that we don't get lured by the transient pleasures of this world; a heavenward gaze which helps us endure when there's opposition. We're called to look to the forerunner of our faith: Jesus, our trailblazer who gave the example of determination to persevere for just a little while knowing that the glory was just around the corner. We read of the same insistent urgency to be like-minded, to be sacrificial in the way we live, from Paul.

Therefore, I urge you, brothers, in view of God's mercy, to offer your bodies as living sacrifices, holy and pleasing to God – this is your spiritual act of worship. Do not conform any longer to the pattern of this world, but be

transformed by the renewing of your mind. Then you will
be able to test and approve what God's will is – his good,
pleasing and perfect will.   (Rom. 12:1-2)

This commitment comes about by an ongoing decision to live for Christ. It isn't something that just happens without our intention. We're called to be fixed upon a new orientation where the old order of thinking is thrown out along with all the distractions.

I benefited from the focus to do the whole Munro tally as it took me on some trips I wouldn't have chosen due to their lack of challenge or character. The Drumochter Hills (see 'Grampian' map, p. 172), especially those east of the A9, rank highest on my list of the least inspiring being two bumps either end of a dreary plateau. Even the meanings of the Gaelic named summits: 'Cairn of the Curve' and 'The Little Yellow Place' speak of the unspectacular nature of these hills! The Drumochter Hills are somewhat spoilt by having a major transport artery cutting through their very heart with heavy traffic rumbling to and from the capital of the Highlands. Even at the start of the hill climb, half of the ascent has already been made. However unpromising a prospect this may appear, there can be surprises in store. In the Drumochter Hills I experienced my first total 'white-out'.

Faith not sight

The round trip only amounted to eighteen kilometres with a total ascent of just 700 metres for two Munros, taking not much more than five hours to complete. I kept this one for winter when daylight hours were short and set out one March day when snow only lay on the tops. Descending from the second summit, the snow began to fall thick and fast which the wind then whipped up into a blizzard. The ridge was already well covered in snow and with the sky full of snow and cloud, nothing, absolutely nothing could be distinguished, not even the lie of the ground at your feet. It was an eerie sensation in terms of sight, drifting along as if in an out-of-body experience, a wandering spirit in a formless world. But the walking was physical and so unpredictable, causing me to stagger, unable to anticipate the contour of the ground.

There are times in life when we are absolutely dumbfounded. Circumstances about us seem to conspire so as to immobilise us. We just don't know which way to turn, there is no guiding light, no helpful signpost. An often quoted proverb says:

Trust in the Lord with all your heart
And lean not on your own understanding;
In all your ways acknowledge him,
And he will make your paths straight. (Prov. 3:5-6)

In such spiritual white-outs the best we can do is to totally seek the Lord through prayer and be directed by His word. It's about absolute trust in God, of placing our lives totally in His care, of not trying to fathom things out ourselves, of ensuring that we choose to walk with Him, however precarious that may seem, making Him our goal and our desire.

There in the Drumochter Hills, I continued on with map and compass, safe in the knowledge of where I was, although I literally couldn't see a thing, but the compass bearing showed me the way back down below the storm, often, incidentally, contrary to the direction my gut told me to take. These two vital aids: map and compass, enabled me to walk 'blind'. I have since used this experience as an illustration, depicting the importance of the guidance of the Holy Spirit together with reference to the Bible. As Paul puts it in 2 Corinthians 5:7, 'We live by faith, not by sight.'

Life at times throws up unexpected things. We flounder and wonder why everything is hidden and become so discouraged we're tempted to just give up or at best, to despair. We wander in a spiritual no-man's-land asking whether this is all there is? We no longer see the light of the sun and the ground before us is so unpredictable that we stagger and limp along, unseeing. Complaining can develop into bitterness and estrangement. We don't always see clearly; if we did, there would be no need for faith. For such dark times let us be encouraged by these words:

Let him who walks in the dark, who has no light,
Trust in the name of the Lord and rely on his God.
   (Isa. 50:10)

Also the following precept from Romans 12:12 is a handy reminder:

Be joyful in hope, patient in affliction, faithful in prayer.

Situations of discouragement or testing mean we have to hold fast to what we have understood, giving ourselves more earnestly to prayer to seek the One who knows the layout of the ground. It's a matter of taking guidance from the word of God to show the obstacles to avoid, as faith compels us to move tentatively forward, walking in obedience to what we know is true, encouraged by biblical promises and instances of God's past faithfulness. Then comes the assurance of the Spirit, that inner guide who directs our ways mysteriously. I write 'mysteriously' because the sense of being led is more an internal experience of being moved to go in a certain way, but we need to be cautious too, checking this bearing makes sense to what's clearly set out on the map, the Bible.

So both Word and Spirit combine to affirm us in the way. Often, affirmation comes from another wayfarer more experienced and wiser who has been that way before. My Bible tutor once counselled me, quoting V. Raymond Edman, 'Never doubt in the dark what God told you in the light.' Trusting in what God has revealed when human sight is reduced is imperative if we are to spiritually mature.

MEDITATION

'Walking by Faith and not by Sight'

Experiencing a total 'white-out' would be totally unnerving without a map or compass. Have you ever been in a situation where you felt so utterly lost, not knowing which direction to turn?

The hillwalker can find the way by knowing how to use a map and compass. How adept are you in going back to scripture to determine perhaps why you are where you are and heed any possible guidance and instruction in how to move on? How open are you to listening to the prompting of the Spirit? How do you determine it is the Holy Spirit that tells you to follow a certain bearing? We would be foolish to just act on a compass without reference to the map, and therefore a prompting to go in a direction that is contrary to the teaching of scripture is foolish.

Here are a few common reasons why we feel lost and far from God, or when God appears silent and we lack guidance in how to proceed:

- **Not confessing something which we know is wrong and being willing to want to overcome it.** *Meditate on Psalm 32. What does it take to be blessed? Is verse 4 what you are experiencing? Then verse 5 is the remedy. Is verse 7 your perception of God's love after confessing? Is verse 8 a real comfort and a reality?*

- **Overwhelmed by fear and worry.** *Read Psalm 46. Note the attributes and the activity of the Lord in the context of a crisis, list them and appropriate a sense of security in knowing the almightiness of a God who cares.*

- **Thinking that we are the losers in the Christian life.** *Read Psalm 73. Does verse 13 echo your own sentiments? List the things that the psalmist is envious of. The oppressors appear to have the upper hand. Note the turning point in verse 17 – how is the perception changed after this? Verses 21-22 spell out the diagnosis – a bitter spirit. Take heart in the words of faith that follow and allow these to overcome that bitterness.*

- **Struggling with depression.** *Read Psalms 42 and 43 together. These don't present an easy fix but you won't feel alone in the way you feel. It's right to be transparent with God (He knows how you are anyway) and He expects His children to speak to Him about their struggles. Continually seek God and intentionally declare your hope knowing that God will respond.*

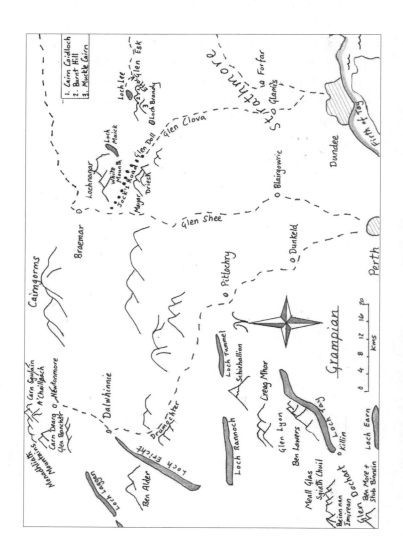

Key:
1. Cairn Caidloch
2. Burnt Hill
3. Muckle Cairn

Loch Lee
Glen Esk
to Forfar
to Glamis
Loch Brandy
Glen Doll
Glen Clova
Loch Muick
Lochnagar
White Mounth
Jock's Road
Muyar Driesh
Braemar
Glen Shee
o Blairgowrie
Dundee
Firth of Tay
Strathmore
Cairngorms
o Pitlochry
o Dunkeld
Perth
Grampian
Carn Gualain
A'Chaillgach
o Newtonmore
Carn Dearg
Glen Banchor
Monadhliath
Dalwhinnie
Loch Tummel
Schiehallion
Creag Mhor
Loch Rannoch
Glen Lyon
Ben Lawers
Drumochter
Loch Ericht
Loch Tay
Loch Earn
o Killin
Meall Glas
Sgiath Chuil
Ben More +
Stob Binnein
Beinn nan
Imirean
Glen Dochart
Ben Alder
Loch Laggan

0 4 8 12 16 20
kms

182

17

On the Trail of Legends

Ben Alder and Glenfinnan

I had set out in the car whilst it was still dark, arriving at Loch Rannoch (see 'Grampian' map, p. 182) just as the last of the stars dwindled in a sky fading from black to grey. The walk began traipsing along lengthy tracks that served the dams of the hydro-electric network in Highland Perthshire. Ben Alder is just one of several remote peaks in Scotland that entail a long day's march or the option of camping to make it more manageable.

To reach just the foot of Ben Alder and return again was like a whole day's excursion in itself of 25 kms – and then to climb the two Munros added a further 13 kms and 960m in height. A storm obscured the two peaks which were separated by a deep saddle, bringing a sense of unease, aware of being far from help. The storm passed and with its clearing, fantastic vistas of the mountainous wilds delighted and urged me on. The autumnal panoramas of the moorland grasses in vivid shades of brown and ochre were exquisite beneath the shifting mists. The moisture-ladened air was often shot with a silvery brilliance caused by sudden moments of sunburst that faded, contrasting dramatically with the newly gathering cloud brooding dark and ready to let loose another storm. It caused you to stop involuntarily in your tracks. This was the landscape of legend, where feats of bravery and endurance against the odds were enacted. This would be the chosen backdrop to convey grandeur that a director of an epic film would wait days for just to shoot, to stun cinema audiences on the big screen.

This great walk into a vast and roadless interior, and the views gradually emerging with the ascent of Ben Alder, provided another fascinating dimension to hillwalking. It's an appreciation of an entire surrounding topography, of being able to piece together the whole land of Highland Scotland through a series of adventures and discoveries that is so beguiling. To look across to another hill range where you have previously walked brings satisfaction, memories and a fresh perspective from which to admire the land under very different weather conditions or even season. It's perhaps something akin to the pleasure of putting in a new piece of a complex jigsaw that suddenly develops and gives fresh clarity to that part of the picture. There's fascination in the lure of neighbouring hills not yet walked. To look upon their steep, dark corries rising dramatically above the remote, windswept wastes of the Highlands does incite some trepidation. The thrill of discovering what remains of the great unknown to you, the anticipation of opening up a fresh expedition that urges you on, provides a new-found zest for life. It ignites a longing for the next outing, the enticement of discovering the next jigsaw piece and that pleasure of fitting it in to see the emerging picture of the whole. The reaching of remote Munros takes you into areas inaccessible by car, train or boat, introducing views otherwise unseen. It's this growing intimacy with the whole land that is one of the most enduring reasons to do the round of all the Munros.

Thirst for the Bible

This matter of desiring to know the whole landscape is rather like the thirst in wanting to know the Bible. We can experience such a real hunger, an appetite whetted by some tasty starter of what we have read, yearning for the main dish, wanting to know God better, that we set aside a day or longer just to read and mull over the words as we digest. In the early years, great hunger drove me to become familiar with the Bible; an enthusiasm that makes me question why the same appetite isn't always there now. To compensate, I find it helpful to set a big block of time aside from time to time to read a whole Bible book along with a commentary and a notebook. Of course this can be done in dribs and drabs through the weeks when studying something the length of the book of Isaiah, but the benefit of doing it at one sitting certainly keeps the big picture in view. An uninterrupted time of being 'away' is so commendable to aid growth, understanding and fruitfulness in the Christian life. Whether this being 'away' is just an intentional time of shutting yourself up in your room ignoring the phone, switching off your mobile and computer, and dispensing with the usual things of life like shopping or domestic chores, even of cooking and eating; or whether it's intentionally going away to a remote place like the Isle of Rum for a long weekend – this is so beneficial in regaining right perspective.

Rum, Eigg or Canna are all such examples of isles well served by ferry that are not far out in the Hebridean Sea but are off the usual tourist trail, where you can find great silence and few distractions and be overawed by the grandeur of nature and exposure to the mighty Atlantic. Such a retreat provides both commentary and reflection on our lives: where we are going, making sense of recent events and of perhaps coming to terms with a recent bereavement, redundancy, health scare, relationship breakdown or other such shock.

This kind of intense searching or 'retreat' doesn't seem to be commended so much these days. There's a gathering tendency to make do with the scraps – a scrap of five minutes of time, a small survival ration of reading a verse or two. It is certainly better than nothing and keeps us spiritually alive, but I would suggest not spiritually vibrant if that is the sum total of our study discipline. And why is this so? More than ever we seem busy with so much to do, not only at work, but in the way we lead our leisure lives. Even church can be at the heart of driving an increasing busyness meaning that we cease to stand still, to listen to the still quiet voice of the Lord that is shut out by the noise of our commotion.

Man of history

On the map written beneath Ben Alder's twin peak appear the tantalizing words: 'Prince Charlie's cave' – a place of refuge in a very remote place. It makes you imagine what could possibly have induced a prince to sleep in a cave, in the days before the popularity of hillwalking and even the concept of the wilds being romantic? I knew something about the tragic debacle of Culloden, the lurid tales of 'the Butcher'- Cumberland – who commenced a callous extermination of any Highlander offering hospitality to the fugitive. An abrupt end to position, estate and even life was the outcome for any Jacobite sympathiser implicated in the flight of the prince. With those words on the map, and standing there in person in that extreme remoteness, it made me want to know more about the Young Pretender to the throne. Maps excite and coming across one tracing the prince's escape after Culloden, totally intrigued me as to the amazing course the flight took. Flight it was, not a preconceived route, but one that responded to the necessities and dire needs of the moment – a serpentine route running south from Culloden, through remote glens and crossing the wild passes of much of north-west Scotland en route to and from the Inner and Outer Hebrides. It enticed one to read the circumstances and the exploits of this desperate escape, the massive manhunt that mobilised an army and navy to track down the hapless prince.

Whatever the convictions held as to the justness or otherwise of the Jacobite cause, it is not a matter upon which I want to comment here. Putting bias aside, I admire the daring of the young prince to raise the Jacobite standard at Glenfinnan (see 'Lochaber' map, p. 148) and stake the Stuart claim to the throne and embark on the overthrow of the Hanoverian crown with only a handful of supporters. What conviction to push on despite the disappointment in the low uptake rallying to his cause! A lesser person would have given up or waited and lost the momentum for action. Many would classify the prince's advance on the government's military garrisons of Stirling and Edinburgh as ill-conceived, desperate, even insane. And yet due to his pugnacity, he overcame the odds and nearly succeeded in achieving his ultimate quest, no doubt borne on by his never-say-die attitude and the early successes of his campaign in defeating and driving the government troops out of Scotland. The Jacobites reached the long road to Derby and had the King in London troubled enough to be preparing his barge on the Thames for a possible escape to Hanover – that's how audacious a quest the Young Pretender had set his heart upon and seemed close to fulfilling at the zenith of his successes.

I walked from the Jacobite monument at the head of Glenfinnan on another Munro expedition, troubled at the outset by thoughts of leading my first conference for Latin Link (a mission organisation operating to and from Latin America that I had newly come to represent). For two years without a coordinator for the mission's work in Scotland, things had fallen into abeyance. Nine months into the position I had little to show for the efforts I had poured into the work, in fact only one student had been sent on a summer team! Not a great start, that hardly encouraged boldness. I walked the estate road towards the base of the summits without great enthusiasm and with a heavy heart. And then the morning light broke on the frozen summits, transforming their heavy ashen masses to peaks ablaze with fiery light. As I climbed, I looked back and pictured the monument in the distance, recalling that at the start of the prince's career, things looked bleak, far from encouraging and the quest to seize the throne an outright impossibility with so few rallying to the standard. And yet he went boldly, undeterred and hopeful – prerequisites surely in pursuing any endeavour.

I was inspired. That weekend after the two Munros climbed mid-week, I asked our small body of thirty-five attendees at the conference to trust and pray that come the following summer, we would have a full team of twelve to send to serve on projects in Latin America. Someone cautioned that we were exceeding our reach. Sure we were. So was Bonnie Prince Charlie. In the words of Robert Browning, 'Ah, but a man's reach should exceed his grasp, or what's a heaven for?' ('Andrea del Sarto', line 98).

Nothing is achieved without gutsy determination. Moreover there is also a whole faith principle to be reckoned with:

> *If you have faith as small as a mustard seed, you can say to this mountain, 'Move from here to there' and it will move. Nothing is impossible for you.* (Matt. 17:20-21)

In fact without such determination and faith, there's no point in pursuing any great endeavour and lack of it would have us settling for mediocrity or dabbling with the small and petty, inconsequential things in life. 'Without faith, it is impossible to please God' are challenging words from the book of Hebrews 11:6. C.T. Studd declared, 'Christ does not want nibblers of the possible, but grabbers of the impossible.'[1]

No wonder the church often looks unattractive as it nibbles away at just what humanly is possible and no more. God honours faith. He didn't just inspire twelve to apply the following year for Latin Link's summer teams, but seventeen from Scotland – a huge boost to morale from a God delighting in answering prayer and working with a vision based on a faith bigger than human possibilities.

---

1. Norman P. Grubb, *C.T. Studd, Cricketer and Pioneer* (Alresford, England: CLC International [UK], June 1985), p. 153.

Greater by far than the determined endeavours of the prince, was the faithfulness of the Highlanders. A ransom of £30,000 was on the head of the fugitive prince and not one of the many people who knew of his whereabouts, with the exception of one, gave his location away. Such honour is commended:

> *A man of many companions may come to ruin,*
> *But there is a friend who sticks closer than a*
>   *brother.*   (Prov. 18:24)

The most famous example of the many who helped the prince was of course Flora MacDonald who had the prince disguised as her maid and went over the sea to Skye as in the words of the famous song. Flora told the Duke of Cumberland – victor of Culloden – when she was later held in captivity in London that she acted from charity and would have helped the Duke himself were he in defeat and in distress.

What faithfulness to risk imprisonment, execution and the confiscation of home and land (and many did), for a man even if not for his cause. It should surely inspire us to lay our all for great enterprises today and vault above the trifling ambition of self-advancement and the love of ease. But the backlash exacted by the government forces was so great that the Highland way of life forever changed. One could argue that it were better had the Highlanders turned in the Young Pretender and spared their way of life. But should the blame be on the complicity of the Highlanders and not on the barbaric methods employed by the Duke of Cumberland? For me, definitely the fine reputation of the Highlander reads the most heroic, far outshining what became the desperations of a prince which ultimately led to an inglorious exile in Rome, characterised by dissipation and oblivion for the remainder of his life. It's unclear how greatly the prince esteemed such sacrificial loyalty, but there is a King who does take note and says, 'Well done, good and faithful servant!' (Matthew 25:21).

Jonathan is a fine biblical example of such solidarity and selflessness, the most faithful of friends in standing up for David, destined by God to take the throne that would have been Jonathan's. David too exemplified great faithfulness towards King Saul even though the king tried to hunt him down and kill David, he refused to exact revenge even when he had the opportunity to put an end to his assailant. We note how God honoured David's principles and even made the wicked Saul declare, 'Because you considered my life precious today, I will not try to harm you again. Surely I have acted like a fool and have erred greatly' (1 Samuel 26: 21).

MEDITATION

'On the Trail of Legends'

To whom do we compare ourselves? Do we look to the hall of fame of the heroes of faith in Hebrews 11? The writer of Hebrews exhorts us:

> *Therefore, since we are surrounded by such a great crowd of witnesses, let us throw off everything that hinders and the sin that so easily entangles, and let us run with perseverance the race marked out for us. Let us fix our eyes on Jesus, the author and perfecter of our faith, who*

for the joy set before him, endured the cross scorning its shame. (Heb. 12:1)

If we look to one another and console ourselves with the thought that we're no less spiritually impoverished than the person next to us in church, we won't aspire to much. If we're not targeting the bull's-eye, we're less likely to hit it or be near to its mark. The heroes of the faith are people just like us as James reminds us (5:17). Scripture is transparent, recording faults and failings which reassure us that God will warm to us when we are spiritually in earnest; He will not abandon us when we get things wrong. The Hebrews 12 quote above incites us to look to Jesus as we persevere through the struggles and misunderstandings of life. Don't grow weary, life is a little breath in the context of eternity and so endure this brief while for the goal of a life without end in God's presence, without suffering and injustice. Therefore keep a heavenly perspective in mind whenever the earthly drags us down – that is the summary of 2 Corinthians 4:16-18:

Therefore we do not lose heart. Though outwardly we are wasting away, yet inwardly we are being renewed day by day. For our light and momentary troubles are achieving for us an eternal glory that far outweighs them all. So we fix our eyes not on what is seen, but on what is unseen. For what is seen is temporary, but what is unseen is eternal.

Do you dare more than you can reasonably achieve? Does your reach exceed your grasp? What could it be that God has been drawing to your attention these past days, months, even years? Examine these afresh – what are the scriptures that support these claims? Are there good reasons why you can't go forward? Consider sharing these thoughts with someone whose spiritual outlook you respect.

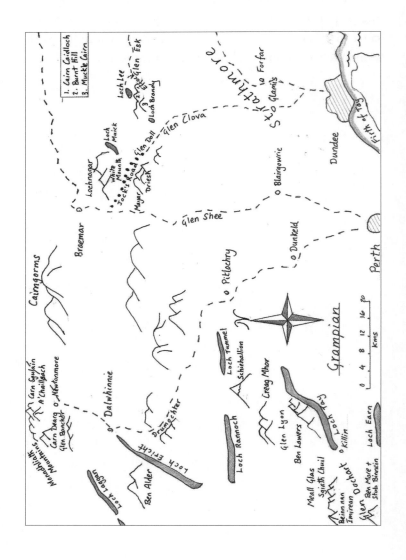

194

18

In Company

Schiehallion, Ben Cruachan, Beinn Eighe, Loch Maree

THE very name 'Schiehallion' (see 'Grampian' Map, p. 194) evokes something fantastical. One of the possible translations of the Gaelic is 'Fairy Hill of the Caledonians'. The fact that it stands apart without a ridge connecting it to the surrounding hills, together with its pyramidal form from some angles, does truly allure many to its summit. Considered Scotland's central peak situated in the very geographic heart of the nation, its highly regular shape was used in an eighteenth-century experiment as a means to calculate the total mass of the earth by noting the deflection of a pendulum caused by Schiehallion's mass. Furthermore, it is Schiehallion that is identified as the holy mountain of the north held in veneration by the Knights Templar as the second Mount Moriah. An inauguration ceremony was held on its slopes during the reign of King Robert the Bruce and some maintain that the king himself was in attendance.

On a few exceptionally clear days, Schiehallion was pointed out to me from Glamis, its fine pyramid appearing across the distance of scores of miles as a small grey shark's fin protruding on the edge of the horizon. After climbing Lochnagar with my head forester, this was next on the list for a joint ascent, a fairy peak on the very outer extremity of his world had been a long held ambition. As Munros go, it is one of the easier due to a road providing access on to its very flank. Its unrelenting path brings you to the summit within two and a half hours, offering an extensive view on a clear day. I've heard that you can see both coasts from this peak, but on my two ascents, the weather was not clear enough.

The second ascent was made with Iain, my son, on a lovely winter's day with total snow cover from the very start. We were the first climbing the hill and not being able to tell exactly where the path lay, we made our own in the virgin snow, thigh deep through the drifts, even up to our waists in one short section. We persevered through to the main ridge, which being windswept, had only a shallow snow layer making for easy going. Later in the day as others came to climb Schiehallion, we felt a certain pleasure seeing everyone following the trail we had blazed before them. To our south beyond the depths of a glen rose the rounded heights of Glen Lyon's Munros, to the north-west Rannoch came in and out of view with the passing cloud and to the north-east Loch Tummel. We sat awhile mesmerised by the grandeur and the great variety of the landscape at our feet, appreciating our achievement in reaching this summit in the depths of winter but feeling it was minisculed by the grand design that lay around us.

*Who has measured the waters in the hollow of his
    hand,
Or with the breadth of his hand marked off the
    heavens?
Who has held the dust of the earth in a basket,
Or weighed the mountains on the scales
And the hills in a balance?* (Isa. 40:12)

Downhill antics

Iain had the habit of flying a small pocket kite from the few Munro summits he joined me on and it flew from Schiehallion's pinnacle for a minute in a rage of a wind before the cord snapped and the kite disappeared down into a corrie. He had adorned the kite with the names of Munros from whose summits it had flown but its loss was soon forgotten as we made a very playful descent, leaping wildly down the ridge and bounding into the drifts with great whoops and wild laughter. Iain was by far the more acrobatic, doing flips and mid-air somersaults in an intense display of exuberance – something that was fairly novel for me as usually being a solitary walker, I didn't dare risk damage to limb by abandoning myself to such antics. Iain inspired me, although probably unwisely for one who had long since lost the suppleness of youth, but the sheer fun remains an abiding memory of a filial bond and I suffered no injury. Those tackling the ascent looked nonplussed by our antics, but had they been on the descent, who knows what reserve they might have flung to the wind!

Just a ridge away from where we now played was where Iain had been suckled as a baby behind a wind-blasted rock. Having largely grown up in the tropics, he now relished everything about the grandeur of the Scottish wilds that we had returned to in his teens. As my father grew a passion for the hills in me, the love was passed on. Iain's preference though is for doing great hill adventures on bikes and these few outings on foot were more a concession on his part to spend time together, something I reciprocated with bike outings into the hills. He felt the comparative limitation of the distance your feet could take you in a day and I was always humbled on bikes, falling behind on the uphill sections. Speeding downhill on bikes passed all too quickly for my liking in an exhilarating blur of absolute speed that challenged skill to remain vertical and on the track, but with no time to appreciate the scenery en route. Both pastimes are excellent in their own way, but we definitely hold to our clear preferences.

On another outing with Iain we were joined by Hannah, my daughter, proving herself very adept at steaming uphill, her slight form seemingly unperturbed by steepness. We had chosen another iconic peak – Ben Cruachan (see 'Mull & Argyll' map, p. 102) – standing rugged and lofty. Having my grown children with me was humbling, as I lacked the speed and agility they so easily displayed. I had once been fleet of foot but here I had to manage a sustainable pace rather than attempt to keep up with my lungs burning and with leaden legs.

One memorable outing with Hannah was climbing Beinn Eighe and its neighbour up in Torridon (see 'Wester Ross' map, p. 80). We had opted for an unconventional shortcut straight up the steep flank from the loch to the summit rather than follow the gentler but much longer loop of the tourist route. In the process we had overtaken a surprised pair of English lads who had been a good distance ahead before we took our shortcut. One of them had the Munro bagging bug whilst his friend was yet to be convinced. The latter, looking at us with an almost inquisitorial air, asked, 'And which way did you come up?' When we indicated our steep and rugged route, he looked at our canvas shoes and said in a most deprecating tone, 'What in those!' It is amusing how superior one person can feel by just wearing the approved kit. We pushed on ahead and later they passed with wry grins as we lunched on the ridge. A little later we passed the one critical of our footwear, now looking much worse for wear, sitting forlorn on a rock in all the right gear. He commented that he was awaiting the return of his mate who had gone on to the second summit, but as for him, he had done quite enough for one day and was ready for the descent. As we ascended the second Munro of the day they started the descent well ahead of us on the approved route. Later on returning to the col where we had last seen them, Hannah and I opted for the scree of another shortcut, bringing us in a mad dash down Beinn Eighe with ski-like finesse. On reaching the path at the bottom of the screes and now nearing the car park, we saw the other two guys on the road a long distance off from the car park.

'Come on, Dad, let's hurry!' Hannah commented as she changed gear to a pace to outstrip them, but without giving the appearance she was belting along. We reached the car park several minutes ahead of them, Hannah relishing the incredulity once more on the face of the outspoken one, as we pulled away in the car. Hannah was chuckling like a drain.

The following day was memorable as we swapped the airy heights of Beinn Eighe for a rowing exploration to Loch

Maree's beautiful islands. We made an eerie landfall on Isle Maree visiting the Viking graves of a prince and princess set within a druid's circle. The pair had both killed themselves owing to an unfortunate timing in a manner akin to Romeo and Juliet.

The saint of the loch

Before the coming of the Vikings was a Celtic saint – Maol Rubha – who gives the loch its name. He had set up a cell upon this island to where presumably he retired and others could seek him out as a notable 'holy man'. Maol Rubha was a great pioneering evangelist in the age of the pagan Picts, travelling extensively bringing the Good News to the isles of Skye and Lewis in the far west and to Forres and Keith in the east. He established a monastery at Applecross which became a great centre of Christianity and Gaelic culture and in his day he and his achievements were considered second in importance to none other than St Columba.

I like the combination that the Celtic missionaries show of brave tenacity to bear a Christian witness in the face of paganism tempered by the need for solitary reflection to keep them truly connected with God. These saints were driven by the concern for the salvation of others and surrendered their own rights, sometimes from princely position too. They sought the audience of kings and warlords requesting permission to bring Christ's light into a world beginning to recognise the dawn of a new age which God was preparing. It is a wonder how the proud race of Picts, 'the last of the free' who had rebuffed the might of Roman rule, should come to embrace a faith and culture alien to their own. Surely it must have been the fear of the Lord.

But God drags away the mighty by his power;
Though they become established, they have no assurance
of life.
He may let them rest in a feeling of security,
But his eyes are on their ways.
For a little while they are exalted, and then they are
gone;
They are brought low and gathered up like all others;
They are cut off like ears of corn.   (Job 24:22-24)

Theirs was an age of uncertainties, where the strong prevailed for a little while, where the old order was contested to make way for the new men of the day. There were rival powers both from within and beyond the land of the Picts that threatened, who sometimes conquered and oppressed, causing the payment of tribute. There were also the other usual uncertainties: health and old age, alliances made and unmade. In those times even warlords and kings will have recognised their mortality and frail hold on life and feared.

Though his pride reaches to the heavens
And his head touches the clouds,
He will perish for ever, like his own dung;
Those who have seen him will say, 'Where is he?'
Like a dream he flies away, no more to be found,
Banished like a vision of the night.
The eye that saw him will not see him again;
His place will look on him no more.   (Job 20:6-9)

When granted land by the regional Pictish ruler the Celtic saints set to work with great energy to create places of learning and refuge, establishing monasteries and cells, holding out a message of salvation and heavenly power which attracted Picts concerned for the welfare of their souls. And their message was seemingly accredited by signs and wonders which later biographers writing hagiography exaggerated and distorted to establish a saint's worthy credentials according to the dictates and fashion of their day. The modern reader dismisses the supernatural, but who is to say there weren't acts of the Spirit to supply this message with power and bring conviction just as we read of in the book of Acts? This was frontier land that the gospel light was penetrating. Under such conditions signs and wonders do accompany the pioneers with acts that attest the veracity of the message, causing a wave of belief, tempered by the opposition from the old order reluctant to give up its hold.

We note another characteristic of these Celtic saints. They were a people of prayer who followed Jesus' example noted in the gospels. Jesus frequently sought out places of solitude to commune with the Father. This felt need to seek out places of quietness and retreat took them often to islands, a quiet refuge from the busyness of their enterprises to give themselves to prayer and contemplation, to maintain a heavenly perspective on current events and needs, and attain godly priorities.

I wait for the Lord, my soul waits,
And in his word I put my hope.
My soul waits for the Lord
More than watchmen wait for the morning
More than watchmen wait for the morning.
  (Ps. 130:5-6)

Vision and prayer

It seems a lesson we would do well to emulate where more than ever progressive churches are so filled with activity in carrying out their programmes and schemes but are often lacking in the need for prayer. Many churches struggle to attract members to prayer meetings and that being the case, we risk cutting ourselves off from the source of godly vision, priorities and attending power. Our Celtic missionary forefathers held that powerful combination of vision that they executed with zeal and of the need to retreat to remain centred on God's purpose and agenda. In that quiet place of prayer and seclusion, they grew strong for the next venture. Scotland and beyond became Christian through these hardy Celtic saints in a most turbulent time of wars.

We left the tall silent larch and 'eternal' holly trees of Isle Maree, and made a boggy landfall on the largest isle, heading inland to view a small lochan in the centre with an equally small island on it. It makes a disputable boast of being the only instance of its kind in all of Europe of an isle on a loch, on an isle on a loch, on an isle in the sea! Its more plausible and rather less romantically put claim is that it's the only island on a loch to have its own lochan and isle. We explored many inlets and lagoons, rowing through the reed grown shallows to follow passages meandering between the isles with rocky gulleys overhung with fine Caledonian pine unharvested over the decades.

The place was so magical that I took a group of five students to these isles for a half day's break during a mission weekend in Gairloch. The students had joined me to work with local churches sharing their testimonies of serving projects and communities in South and Central America through Latin

Link. When possible, I liked to combine bringing their youthful enthusiasm for Christ and His mission to inspire local rural churches, with doing something adventurous. The combination gave the name to these church tours as 'Mission Adventures', providing a way for me to get to know each short-term returnee much better. They had the effect of iron sharpening iron as they inspired one another afresh with their shared mission experience and conviction.

The rowing trip with the students was unfortunately in the rain and we had to walk the wetlands of the largest island to view 'the isle on a loch, on an isle on a loch, on an isle in the sea'. I had perhaps overstated the charm of my earlier visit with Hannah for when we had traipsed through all the bog, pursued by every midge in the Loch Maree area to peer through the mist of falling rain at this tiny isle on a lochan, one of the young lads remarked, 'I would like to say that I'm impressed!' We returned to the boats and were much relieved when the midges decided they wouldn't join us out on the loch.

The rain reduced to a drizzle and spirits weren't exactly hyper as lunchtime approached. The idea had been to picnic on one of the islands, but the midges put pay to that idea and now we were faced with the prospect of eating in a couple of rowing boats subdued beneath a heavy and still dripping overcast sky.

'Let's have a floating picnic,' I announced as I brought our boat alongside the other, placing the two sets of oars together across the boats to form a kind of table. On to this our considerable picnic was laid out. The 'floating picnic' was just the thing, so novel that none had heard of it before. All the food goodies lifted our spirits as we passed pies and pieces, olives and cake across the two boats drifting between two islands and by the time we had done, it had stopped raining altogether.

Later that day we had a bonfire and barbeque on a beach with the youth from around Gairloch. Our group spoke of authentic mission experiences in various Latin American countries where their view of Christ had been made the more real. Faith and expectation had been considerably heightened by the mission experience as when they came to the end of their own resources, offering to God their small acts of service often produced a big blessing for local communities. The Gairloch youth listened well and took these things to heart. The following day, Sunday, brought three more opportunities for the group to share and help run the local worship services in Gairloch, Poolewe and Aultbea. Every generation expressed how they felt encouraged by us coming to their out-of-the-way place and our small team were touched by the generosity of spirit and graciousness of everyone they encountered. The weekend was as memorable as the many other 'Mission Adventures'.

MEDITATION

'In Company'

Recollections of some playful and memorable outings with my children stand out. Recall some of your memorable times with others in the hills or when doing something together outdoors has helped you connect with another. Give thanks for these. Consider the elements that made the time special, mindful too of not forgetting to pass on the blessing to others you may take to the hills in the future.

The early Celtic monasteries were more Christian communities than strict monastic orders associated with the medieval period. These communities were lights in a dark age, where men and women could find refuge and be instructed through word and example, and through prayer they found the fellowship in the trinity. With whom do you find spiritual refreshment and encouragement? Who are you accountable to?

A rowing outing to Isle Maree made me aware of Saint Maol Rubha. He was a man of energy and vision who recognised the need to retire to his solitary island to remain connected with his Father and not to allow the busyness to run away with him or to run ahead of the Lord in his own energy.

How much of an activist are you? What importance do you place on prayer in the busy scheme of things? Do you draw aside from the bustle to reflect, to review what's passed before the Lord, in order to gain a more heavenly perspective on events, to focus on where God is blessing? This is a necessary exercise to shed some of the less productive activities, otherwise we become consumed with busyness and risk burn-out, or at the very least, become far less connected with God's agenda. Do you seek His counsel in what lies ahead, reluctant to move until assured of His word and purpose? Consider this prayer and then try to make it your own:

Leave me alone with God
As much as may be.
As the tide draws the waters
Close in upon the shore,
Make me an island, set apart,
Alone with you, God,
Holy to you.

Then with the turning of the tide,
Prepare me to carry your presence
To the busy world beyond,
The world that rushes in on me,
Till the waters come again
And fold me back to you.

From *Celtic Daily Prayer* [1]

---

1. *Celtic Daily Prayer* (Marshall Pickering, 1994), p. 167.

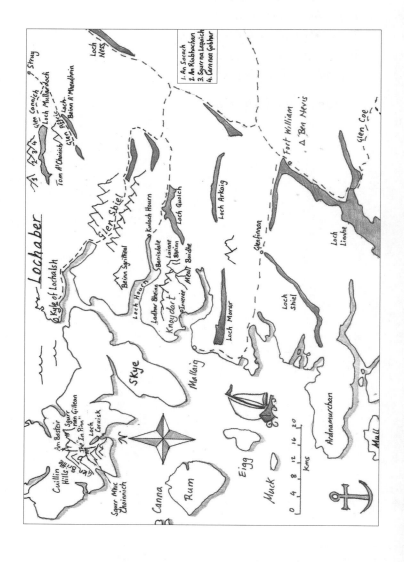

Lochaber

Loch Ness

Glen Cannich   Struy
Loch Mullardoch
Glen Affric
Tom A'Choinich   Loch
Beinn A'Mheadhoin

1. An Socach
2. An Riabhachan
3. Sgurr na Lapaich
4. Carn nan Gobhar

Fort William
△ Ben Nevis
Glen Coe

Kyle of Lochalsh

Glen Shiel

Beinn Sgritheall

Loch Hourn
Kinloch Hourn

Loch Arkaig

Ladhar Bheinn   Barrisdale
Knoydart   Luinne Bheinn
Inverie   Meall Buidhe

Loch Quoich

Glenfinnan

Loch Lochy

Skye

Cuillin Hills
Sgurr nan Gillean
An Basteir
Mhic Gilleann
The In Pinn
Loch Coruisk

Sgurr Mhic Choinnich

Loch Morar

Loch Shiel

Mallaig

Canna

Rum

Eigg

Muck

Loch Linnhe

Ardnamurchan

Mull

0 4 8 12 16 20
Kms

19

Plans Frustrated

Knoydart

THE Knoydart peninsula (see 'Lochaber' map, p. 208) has the charm of an island, only better! Inaccessible by car and requiring a two-day commitment back in 2009 just to visit this part of the country due to the infrequency of the passenger ferry, this places Knoydart firmly off the tourist trail for most. Those wishing to take in huge swathes of Scotland in search of out-of-the-way, rugged charm are most likely to choose nearby Skye for accessibility; a region synonymous with mountainous west coast scenery and celebrated in song.

Knoydart is encompassed by sea on three sides and far from any road end. Its three Munros involve a stay of a couple of nights for most hillwalkers and that was the plan on arriving with my daughter, Hannah. We were met at the Inverie pier by a Land Rover, courtesy of the estate through whom we had booked a couple of bunks at The Barn, a gesture much appreciated as we were laden with provisions for our long weekend.

We set out the following morning along the estate track in the direction of the pass to Barrisdale with plans to climb Ladhar Beinn. I hadn't felt too good on setting out but had hoped this might pass as I established my pace. But my weariness grew and we had to call a halt at Loch an Dubh-Lochain and whiled away the morning wistfully viewing the hills rising on the far shore of the loch before inspecting the substantial ruins of a former cottage and steading.

There are so many ruins, abandoned shielings and disused sheep fanks in the Scottish hills giving a melancholic air to glens that were once well populated. The people had known these hills far more intimately than any Munroist and had named the peaks and glens, rivers and lochs, even modest looking burns. Knoydart used to have a population of 1,000 people before the Highland Clearances, but by the end of the nineteenth-century, the population was reduced to just fifty. Evidence from the past lies about in the tumbled stones for those who choose to stare and to wonder. What tales these dressed stones could tell from the time the stone-mason had selected and shaped them, to their builders and the generations who lived within their walls. What sorrowful tales could be told in their abandonment, many evicted in the 'Clearances', others driven out by famine, or lured by easier ways to make a living in the fast industrialising Glasgow, or further afield in the New World. The stones' silence is poignant and cannot help but tug at the heartstrings when considering generations of Highlanders from Pictish times right through to just a few generations back, who didn't travel beyond a small radius from their homesteads except for the seasonal migration to the summer shielings in the higher hill pastures. This was all they knew of the world and everything around them was named as their point of reference.

The following day I felt much the same – extreme lethargy, perhaps some souvenir brought back from years spent in the tropics, as every so often a bout of extreme weariness passes over me and stays for two or three days then is gone.

Remote moments

That weekend we had The Barn to ourselves and we enjoyed reading and reminiscing and delving into the visitor's book. One entry read, 'Today we saw the elephant of Knoydart!' A page or two later, one stickler for the facts wrote emphatically, 'There are no elephants in Knoydart!' But then a page or so on, some impish visitor teasingly wrote, 'We saw the elephant of Knoydart this evening!' We noticed at the pub, boasting to be the remotest inn on mainland Britain, that Knoydart drew in its share of eccentrics and colourful characters: artists, ageing hippies, and ecologists setting up an estate run by the community intent on developing its natural habitat. The remoteness and the very quintessence of wild Scotland draws in those in search of an antidote to this convenience age of rolling up in your car outside the door of your tourist board graded accommodation. It reminds me of the lines from Kenneth Steven's *Garve* lamenting about the passing of the indigenous Gaelic speaker world:

They have all blown away,
The ones who knew these hills by name,
Who translated the wind, who spoke
The same language as the curlew.

I remember
The day I came here in childhood
To watch the last of my mother's people buried
Under a weight of memories and snow.

They are replaced by foreign bodies
With Range Rovers and mobile phones,
Who smooth the road to London in a day
And do not care.'

Garve[1] – from a collection of poems entitled
Iona – Kenneth Steven

We left the peninsula enchanted by its laid-back style. True – no Munros had been added to the tally, but calm acceptance is a gift when we don't presume we can just do exactly as we would wish, where force and circumstance intervene. Some would feel very frustrated by such an outcome, and I have to own to times of feeling that myself when things lose perspective, usually as a result of trying to squeeze so much into so small a space of time and being frustrated when things don't transpire in the way we would wish. My daughter and I had a fine time making our own entertainment and came away feeling more rounded by the experience. We often reminisce on this special place kept aside from the world and held in such a fondness that Hannah chose it a couple of years later for her wedding celebrations combined with her departure to a new life in America. Her wedding invitation was home-made, a hand drawn map rather pirate-like, sent complete with a compass for the intrepid few to use to find this remote inn. Distance, a fishing-boat ferry that made it difficult for the not so able to board, together with the anticipation of foul weather at the summer's end, kept some from coming.

---

1. *Garve.* From collection entitled 'Iona' (Edinburgh: Saint Andrew Press, 2000), p. 3.

Those who rose to the adventure were rewarded by an Indian summer, dawn to dusk sunshine, with temperatures so relatively high that the young folk I had taken to a waterfall deep into the hills stripped off to bathe in the inviting pool at its feet.

The next trip to Knoydart was on my own with a tent, coming in from the north-east from Kinloch Hourn. This was my first trip camping, as up until then I had always managed long day marathons sometimes assisted by bike, but these three Munros in a day and back out again exceeded my capabilities. By the time I had reached Barrisdale about ten kilometres later, I regretted bringing so many provisions, half of which I carried out again, teaching me the lesson to have a meal plan and to strictly provide only for that, resisting the temptation to throw in all manner of snacks and additional meals just in case I was hungrier than anticipated.

The path to Barrisdale is a delight as it starts from the very head of Loch Hourn, the water narrow and the hills steep on either side. The early stages are through rhododendrons and under old pines through which the views north to the hills across the loch are memorable; the path rising and falling with the habit of surprising with a new view, all the while following the tidal loch toward the open sea.

En route I recognised a man I had spoken with a week earlier on the summit of Liathach, when we discovered we were both down to our final ten Munros. He had set off from Kinloch Hourn in the early hours of the day, did the round of three and was heading back to base again mid-evening; a trip of 47 kms and total height climbed of 1,900 m amongst some of the most rugged terrain in Scotland. As these figures clearly state, he was super fit from spending three months living in a small camper van, doing daily sorties. Presumably climbing becomes mechanical and a good deal less effortless when you're daily on the hill. He was saving until last Ben More on Mull in order to climb it with his wife, providing a fine destination for some holiday together. A man of similar age to myself he was in buoyant mood, saying that he had given up on various things in life, but this was something significant he had persevered with and was therefore of great significance to him. This man also humorously told me about hitching a lift to help him complete the seven Munros on the south side of Glen Shiel. The only vehicle to stop was one of those machines that painted white lines down the centre of the road. He mounted on to the back, sat on top of the paint tank and proceeded tediously slowly up Glen Shiel.

The ascent of Ladhar Beinn from Barrisdale up into its northern corries is an exhilarating walk. Alighting on to the well-trodden zigzag path from the level marshes across the sea inlet from Barrisdale is a relief and takes you over a spur into the glen proper beyond, remote and brilliant under the sun picking out the cascades of a swift mountain burn. Beyond rise the pathless steep braes soaring up on to the undulating and broken summit ridge. This is the highest point of the peninsula and the views take in Skye to the west and Beinn Sgritheall, another isolated Munro, to the north across Loch Hourn. The view back east into the heartland of Knoydart is much more austere, dominated by the neighbouring Munros of Luinne Bheinn and Meall Buidhe with their extensive eruptions of rock without turf making this a desolation of rock. That view made me take stock and realise that to attempt all three Munros that day was perhaps over ambitious. In younger days maybe I would have been up for it. But hillwalking had become much more than a physical feat and if you are to take in the views and savour the atmosphere and allow these to shape your mood, then walks shouldn't be rushed. If quietness of spirit is the goal then sometimes it means settling for less.

Time to consider

However, what I didn't expect was another dose of the lethargy that had hit me previously with Hannah and kept us to base around Inverie. This came upon me halfway out from camp, making it a challenge just getting back, even though most of the way was downhill. It saved me the conundrum of whether to include at least one other Munro that day, as the shortest route back became the new goal. Stupidly I didn't check the map when coming over the ridge between Ladhar Beinn and the Barrisdale-Inverie cross-peninsula track. I started a descent down a very steep ridge broken with many rock scrambles that put me into an increasingly compromising situation. In craggy hills it's imperative to consult the map for a safe route and it saves the humility of being wrong and the long arduous toil of backtracking uphill. It's rather allegorical. We often end up in a mess when we don't think before we act and plunge into some decision without reference to any wise counsel, prayer or experience. It's often born out of impatience, a sudden need or desire. It makes us wise to the need to take time to consider, time to consult and derive direction which time in prayer often provides for.

I still had a long part of the day remaining as I rested up in the entrance of my wee tent facing the very pointed peak of Aonach Sgoilte – Ladhar Bheinn's neighbour – outrageously steep, towering over the glen where I had almost come undone had I not returned to its summit. That afternoon and evening were very solitary on the flat end of Barrisdale, settled first by the Vikings who had named it. A rare flat valley in a wilderness of mountain and crags and rocky shores must have been so inviting to those Norse seafarers in search of farmable land. The random notes of skylarks woven with the wind in the grass produced a sense of great detachment, melancholy and an appreciation of such solitude. It evoked both a loneliness and gladness to be alive as I reminisced on climbing the unique Ladhar Bheinn.

The next day's intention to tackle the remaining two Munros was again frustrated by health, thus bringing a tally of only one Munro from two outings that in all had taken up six days! Such delayed progress would have been tantamount to despair had this been more common. We can but plan and hope and try to succeed but the outcome isn't always within our control and there's peace in recognising that:

> *The race is not to the swift*
> *Or the battle to the strong,*
> *Nor does food come to the wise*
> *Or wealth to the brilliant or favour to the learned;*
> *But time and chance happen to them all.* (Eccles. 9:11)

Acknowledging that we're not always in control isn't defeatism, but engenders a healthy respect for the hills. We don't automatically conquer, for sometimes they conquer us. Setbacks raise the stakes for the next outing, which in turn enhances the achievement when we do finally succeed. It's salutary that my more memorable outings are these very ones when the gain did not come easily.

The third and final outing to Knoydart was a return to Inverie on the Mallaig boat. I had two backpacks, the larger one with tent and a change of clothes as well as supper and breakfast was left tucked under rhododendrons near the edge of a forest for my return. So I proceeded with my small backpack, setting my sights on those two elusive peaks. It was already midday when I arrived at the pier and I had plans to be on the next day's ferry back again. This time my health didn't let me down, but the weather did. It turned foul and so very wet and windy that I saw very little up on the heights. The traverse of the dereliction of vast rock eruptions wasn't as bad as I had expected and I was thankful. By early evening I had made the track at the pass between Barrisdale and Inverie. The rain had stopped but my wet trousers were chafing me sore. Still it was very notable to have finally made it to the tops of these two hard-to-reach Munros and be ambling at an enjoyable pace downhill, enjoying the views of the cloud lifting from the hills and sunbeams bursting through at times to light up the glen before me. This brightening epitomised my own mood of extreme satisfaction at having completed the big three of Knoydart. That night I slept in the forest, well content to be in dry clothes and in a warm sleeping-bag, dining on an unsquashed sandwich for my supper. It felt homely, all that I needed, not wishing anything to be different – something that appeals to the primal instincts yet inherent in us if only we would push the boundaries and explore. It's all too easy to settle for the familiar, to abide with the status quo and by no design to end up in something of a rut. The Munros caused me to raise my game, to build up stamina through making increasingly longer hikes in preparation of the epic trips; opening up the delight of new experiences like carrying camp to relish an evening of still solitude in the hills.

MEDITATION

'Plans Frustrated'

When illness or lack of energy cause us to fail in what we have set out to achieve, how do we respond? Are we able to overcome the disappointment and frustration? Are we crushed and angry? Do these emotions fester until we have overcome? How accepting of failing are we – does it have a purpose? We need to be philosophical about such things and remember that we're not the absolute master:

> *The race is not to the swift*
> *Or the battle to the strong,*
> *Nor does food come to the wise*
> *Or wealth to the brilliant or favour to the learned;*
> *But time and chance happen to them all.* (Eccles. 9:11)

We seem so programmed to achieve, to conquer that when we fail we find it hard to come to terms with it. There is a certain pride and arrogance in such an attitude that we need to check. We don't have the right to always succeed in any enterprise we put our hands to. 'He has blocked my way so that I cannot pass' (Job 19: 8). We don't have the right to live to threescore years and ten. We are under God and He determines these things, not us. In all things we need to acknowledge Him and be accepting of circumstances beyond our control and take heart that we are in God's care and under His rule.

Can you fathom the mysteries of God?
Can you probe the limits of the Almighty?
They are higher than the heavens – what can you do?
They are deeper than the depths of the grave – what
*   can you know?*
Their measure is longer than the earth and wider than
*   the sea.* (Job 11:7-9)

When success comes it's not solely our doing: 'To him belong strength and victory' (Job 12:16). God has given strength and wisdom and orchestrated circumstance. We don't conquer, but rather He has enabled us to overcome the odds. When we fail, then there's another day when success will be all the sweeter and we will be the better for it: 'When he has tested me, I shall come forth as gold' (Job 23:10).

Read one stanza of Psalm 119:65-72. Note how the Lord uses affliction to lead us back to Himself. According to verse 67 what happens when we have everything our way? Consider the things that have beset us. Can we also say with the psalmist in verse 71, 'It was good for me to be afflicted so that I might learn your decrees.'

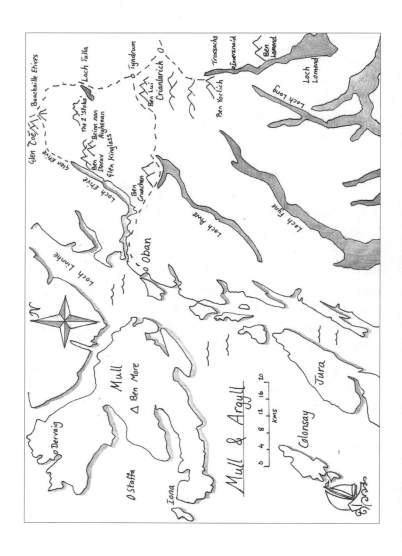

220

20

Weathering the Storm

Glen Etive and Glen Cannich Hills

ALL through mid-summer, a dark unbroken cloud enveloped the peaks around Glen Etive (see 'Mull & Argyll' map, p. 220), moving in a threatening 'off-limits' manner along the ridges. The light was all subdued in what I have always considered a dramatic glen of contrasts. Certainly the usual charm was absent and it hardly seemed the place I remembered with the rhododendrons in full bloom around the fringe of a lochan, interspersed with larch and Scots Pine. A finer picnic spot would be hard to find, with its grand backdrop of the twin Buachaille Etives standing sentinel at the head of the glen like two neatly formed pyramids and between them an exquisitely symmetrical V-shaped valley pass, creating a picture-perfect scene.

But today upon arrival one wasn't inspired to dash out of the car and on to the hills, such was their brooding manner verging on the menacing. However, if you limited yourself to fine weather climbing there would be a good deal of aborted expeditions. Besides working full-time doesn't allow you to be choosy but to accept what the weather might bring, which is a good thing too, because different weather certainly makes you resolve to persevere, in turn shaping character. I had five Munro summits in my sights that day, first on the list – Ben Starav – presenting an unrelenting steep flank rising from sea level at Loch Etive all the way to its peak hidden in the billowing cloud.

Tackling the first peak of many planned for the day is a sobering experience, especially when all of the 1078 metres had to be climbed. It removes the cockiness from your stride, makes you wonder with a further four summits ahead whether you have bitten off more than you can chew. The wind was up on the peak, screeching raw over the screes and boulders and visibility was not much more than fifty feet, necessitating walking by compass all day long from ridge to ridge.

Such hesitant sentiments are experienced when starting out in a new job, or learning a new task, a foreign language or skill. You do question your ability. You do wonder whether you can succeed. And what had at first seemed inspiring and led you to try such a thing, now fills you with concern so that you feel audacious to have thought you could have been up for such a challenge. The initial experience can make you think of cutting your losses. The speed it takes to reach the top is not so important. Whether you stop frequently or crawl like a snail; making it to the pinnacle is an achievement, proving you can do it. You feel stronger for not giving in and in overcoming the doubt; you gain more confidence.

Ben Starav was in very different aspect to how I had seen her on my first sighting years before, when my father and I had come to camp the night on the shores of Loch Etive after my aborted attempt to walk all the hill ridges between Lomond and Ben Nevis. We had experienced one of those evenings of great stillness with a deepening gold intensity as the evening matured. The reflections of Ben Starav on the still waters of the sea loch were so mesmerising that neither dared break the spell by talking. I have a framed photo above my desk – a memento from a time when father and son had especially connected – of him sat some distance off upon a boulder by the water's edge enthralled by the grandeur all about him, so caught up and becoming one with it.

In fair weather and foul

A drop of 400 metres brought me to the col east of Ben Starav, followed by a traverse across steep slopes to reach the unsighted bealach north of Beinn nan Aighenan. Only here did the mist part for some twenty seconds revealing a view east down the steep-sided glen, an arm of Glen Kinglass. The burn shone brightly in its silver trail coursing quickly down its dizzy descent to the levelling watershed at the top end of Glen Kinglass and the eastward traverse through to Loch Tulla and Bridge of Orchy. This new territory enthralled me, sowing the idea to travel some of these long, rather inaccessible glens at some later stage, an ambition in this case fulfilled when I walked my own route from St Andrews to Iona and walked the length of Glen Kinglass on part of that coast to coast – something of a personal pilgrimage starting from a major centre of the Reformation back to the beginnings of Christianity in Scotland. Twenty seconds was all that I glimpsed the whole day long of the view, its brevity making it precious. That was the sole reward for a great exertion of much plodding, enduring and trusting the compass, finding ways around the craggy landscape necessitating quite a meandering course at times. My clothes became heavy and tight saturated by the unabating rain and wind, keeping me constantly on the move as it became chilly standing still for just a minute. There have been quite a number of trousers I've got through in such conditions, giving way with a big tear. My wife bought me a Gore-Tex pair that never ripped. But rip me they did which my wife was fine about as she claimed I was self-mending! That pair of indestructible breeks reminded me of the tale of a Viking lord – Ragnar – whose wife made a 'supernatural' pair of trousers from a bear skin rolled in tar and doused in sand to transform them into something fireproof in the event he should ever have to combat a fire-breathing dragon. It earned him the name 'Ragnar the Hairy Breeks'. I can imagine the grief these caused poor Ragnar and wondered whether Mrs Ragnar too had become tired of mending his breeks.

It took dogged determination to do the round of five Munros and you couldn't appreciate the character of the hills for the lack of visibility, making you wonder whether it was all worthwhile. Only on reaching the car exchanging wet clothes for dry ones could I look back at the solid cloud enveloping those five summits, a hidden prize obtained by a mysterious feat. I couldn't confess to having enjoyed the whole experience! It all felt rather too much like a hard discipline, unpleasant at the time, but with just a suggestion that it was beneficial.

Our fathers disciplined us for a little while as they thought best; but God disciplines us for our own good, that we may share in his holiness. No discipline seems pleasant at the time, but painful. Later on, however, it produces a harvest of righteousness and peace for those who have been trained by it. (Heb. 12:10-11)

And that lasting peace is the residue of such endurance in the hills. If we give up all too easily, we just become quitters. We need that persevering spirit in relationships as the difficult times often bring better understanding and the love shows an expression of commitment that can win through the thick and thin of experience. But there are also times when we do need to quit, such as my aborted attempts mentioned on the Skye Cuillin. It takes discretion to know which is appropriate: to carry on or to turn back.

The majority of hill walks I've undertaken were under similar conditions due to walking at the crack of dawn, even pre-dawn if there were a good track to walk in the dark to enable me to be back mid-afternoon to mind the guesthouse business. Walks deep into the Cairngorms from the Caledonian forests of upper Deeside come to mind, of being unnerved in the rutting season by the roar of the unsighted stags sounding nearby in the pre-dawn darkness, hoping not to run into one.

Step by step

The misty and moist hill adventures formed the usual pattern, so much so, that when the weather was fair and views were far-reaching, they became the exception and therefore the more cherished and most noteworthy of inclusion in this tally. This is probably a metaphor for the ordinariness of daily existence that has much to do with the monotony that requires us to just get on with the task, to put on a brave face and to see it through. Very often at the outset with the first lengthy ascent of the day, you battle with questioning whether it is worthwhile and why not give in and try another day. It's often more due to lethargy of spirit than physical fatigue. It takes grit to pull yourself together sometimes amounting to a pep talk and to break a big ordeal into bite size pieces. You view the upward slope ahead and decide where your next breathing point will be and determine that no way will you give in until it is reached. Sometimes you exceed the marked point and you applaud your effort. During the rest, you assess at what contour you might be at by looking at the hills across the glen and reckoning on a position level to your own, and from this can hopefully take some comfort in knowing the height gained and assess the remainder yet to come as being quite manageable. Such ways of encouraging your ascent become an attitude transferable to basic life skills where you break down a big task or long-term goal into realisable pieces. Rather than be so in awe of the epic task, you just have to stop procrastinating and take the first step. Lao-Tzu addresses this very issue in a memorable quote: 'A journey of a thousand miles begins with a single step.' Progress is maybe slow at first, but if it's steady it can be surprisingly quickly accumulative. In all likelihood there will be that moment of breakthrough when what you set your sights upon, at one time seeming out of reach, becomes suddenly feasible and then achievable.

Our spiritual lives are quite similar, although we long for the highs, the times of revelation, of treading the mountain tops, experience is often very different and has too much of the mundane and the drudgery for our liking. Often it is we who are at fault, living compromised lives, unable to overcome bad habits whose appeal is so strong; or when half-hearted in our devotion we're careless of cultivating time with the Lord that we walk, as it were, in the cold cloud, unseeing, stumbling over the screes, missing the right ridge and having to backtrack. These are purging experiences that awaken the need for forgiveness, to be put right and to seek His face afresh.

Cleanse me with hyssop, and I shall be clean;
Wash me, and I shall be whiter than snow ...
Hide your face from my sins and blot out all my
*   iniquity.*
Create in me a pure heart, O God, and renew a
*   steadfast spirit within me ...*
Restore to me the joy of your salvation and grant me a
*   willing spirit to sustain me.*   (Ps. 51:7, 9, 10, 12)

I couldn't help thinking back to that glorious evening years before passed with my father at the foot of Ben Starav. I missed his company. He had imparted so much during my formative years, not only in acquiring this hillcraft, but creating within me this profound appreciation of the majesty of the hills. I felt melancholic, struggling more than usual on account of it.

But having completed the day's ambitious tour, I felt refined by the elements, defying the mist by not losing the way. It had made me a better person, resisting the recurrent nag within to give up and turn back. The ordeal purged any residual arrogance, making me realise afresh how frail our tenure is upon the face of the earth. I felt rejuvenated, having excelled against the odds.

The hills that shaped me

My last Munro outing was chosen with care, one that would be a long-distance sortie deep into the hills far from the public road, an ascent to vast sweeping ridges above lochs and glens unseen before. I didn't want just a single hill, or something so rugged and technical that I couldn't enjoy the rhythm of a long solitary walk. Glen Cannich was the final setting (see 'Lochaber' map, p. 208), starting with a boggy slog along the marshy shore of Loch Mullardoch leading to the far end of the ridge to ascend An Riabhachan – the highest hill in Ross-shire. I had made an outing the previous March to climb the remote and solitary An Socach at the distant end of this ridge in quite challenging Arctic-like conditions with tremendous wind-chill that caused my head to ache with such disturbing violence that anxious to leave the summit, I ran at times faster than my legs could take me, pitching me into a tumble in the snow. That memorable excursion brought an encounter with a solitary walker very early in the morning coming from the north-east, a great distance from any access point. The stranger stopped and loosening his backpack to the ground, shared his home-made chocolate, nut and fruit mix. He explained he had come the previous day from Achnasheen railway station and had camped overnight in the great frozen wilderness between there and Kintail to where he was now making. He stopped only briefly, a solitary, mysterious man almost an angelic visitor. The encounter inspired me later to carry camp (tent, sleeping and cooking equipment) and traverse the great hinterlands that the Munros had introduced me to, to places still remaining only partially known. As I reached the cloud covered summit of An Riabhachan in pensive mood after completing a forty-year campaign to ascend all the Munros, I felt huge fulfilment at reaching the end but also began wondering what was next. Would life lose some thrill now the challenge was complete? Thanks to that solitary wayfarer, new adventures lay ahead, further explorations of the yet-to-be-discovered glens and hills of Scotland and most of the Hebrides that I hadn't set foot upon that I continue to walk to this day. More tests of stamina, more moulding of character, engendering that intimacy with the Creator who put perspective on all my petty concerns, fears and achievements through the grandeur of the hills.

Still the last two Munros lay ahead, eastward above the loch to complete the grand Munro tour. I had half wished the weather to be fine so that I could look in all directions at the myriad hills and recall the many outings that brought me to their summits over the past decades. But no, it was the usual Scottish hill weather, raining and blustery with cloud cover requiring walking unsighted along compass bearings. Just another such day in the hills that had shaped me.

The task complete I drove back to Struy where I had left Alexandra at the inn. This final expedition had also been chosen for this nearby pub to reward the patience of my wife with a good dinner. She had been enjoying reading books and had had a wee saunter around the local lanes earlier in the day. Her day had been good too.

The gift of the Munro guide had set me off on this long quest twenty years earlier. But my wife had also made me the dubious Gore-Tex gift of Ragnar's hairy breeks that I hung up after that final Munro outing and never wore again until I finally donated these to a charity shop. I wonder who chafes in these now? If there was anything heroic about the end of my Munro days then it was deeply imbedded chafing scars that remain to this day that put me in the league with the Viking lord who endured battle in his quasi-supernatural breeks!

I don't tend to go in quest of the summit so much since completing a round of all the Munros, (although I am enjoying climbing some 'Corbetts' – hills of over 2,500 feet – in regions where there are no Munros, for the purpose of becoming familiar with other parts of Scotland). I more relish the long-distance walks of two to three days carrying the necessities in a backpack and with the companionship of my collie, 'Spartikades Keristophanes', which translates into the vulgar tongue, 'Chaser of deer, catcher of none' – (but you know we just call him 'Sparkie' for short when he's not looking noble). So together with Sparkie I enjoy some very special camps in wild and romantic places. This way I have been able to cross considerable swathes of a region, lured on by the distant horizon wondering what lies beyond, appealing to something inherent within us known by our distant ancestors that drove them in search of new hunting grounds or land to cultivate. These far less trodden ways have at times been so off the beaten track that the going has been hard through tussocky grass and heather, something the early Munroists must have encountered requiring more physical perseverance and without the psychological goading on of a well-trodden path. The concentrated time away continues to filter out the noisy distortions that surround our lives until quietness enfolds and the ability to listen and to perceive what is of consequence becomes apparent.

I have moved south of the Highlands to Clackmannan-shire to be more centrally based to most of the major concentrations of population. Working on the 'homeside' of an overseas mission has been a learning process, a considerable adjustment from working in an exotic location where I was blessed to be feeding a hunger for the word of God. My role as Scotland Coordinator is to inspire a closer walk with God in a climate of less spiritual hunger to what I have encountered in the Philippines. I do this partly by sharing with various denominations right across Scotland, and partly by working with individuals and groups who have been out on short-term projects. The most satisfying aspect of my work is in helping to identify the call of God, helping each in some small way to spiritually prepare for environments that are precarious but at the same time are more open to seek God.

MEDITATION

'Weathering the Storm'

Hillcraft is perfected in adverse weather conditions. If we are only fair weather walkers, we're poorly prepared for challenges as in the proverb, 'A smooth sea never made a skilled mariner'. Character is shaped when the going gets tough. Paul wrote:

> *Suffering produces perseverance; perseverance, character; and character, hope. And hope doesn't disappoint us, because God has poured out his love into our hearts by the Holy Spirit, whom he has given us.* (Rom. 5:3-5)

How do we react when the going gets tough? Dogged determination is a discipline, not that pleasant at the time but the benefits are felt at least afterwards. Such an attitude combats lethargy. How easily do you quit? Try the spiritual discipline of standing firm in what might be confronting you at this time, asking for the Father's help to strengthen your hand.

Walking in the cloud, wind and drizzle can be something of a metaphor for the spiritual life – much of it can be humdrum. The experience can feel punitive, possibly indicating that we've strayed from God's standards and from His presence. Often we can be responsible for this through the compromise of giving in to bad habits, when we are half-hearted in our devotion.

If this is an issue, identify what's holding you back from enjoying the spiritual life. Repent, asking God to help you stand up under temptation. This is a repeated exercise which of course we won't entirely win until we get to heaven. Be encouraged though by the times you don't give in and have stood your ground. This is an opportunity for repentance, to mend the broken bond and revive the close fellowship with Christ as experienced around a dinner table.

Those whom I love I rebuke and discipline. So be earnest, and repent. Here I am! I stand at the door and knock. If anyone hears my voice and opens the door, I will come in and eat with him, and he with me. (Rev. 3:19-20)

Be encouraged that it's the Lord who brings the rebuke, that He comes to our home in a gentle manner to remind us so that we may mend our ways, as in the caring manner Jesus showed Zacchaeus, the corrupt tax collector (Luke 19:1-10).

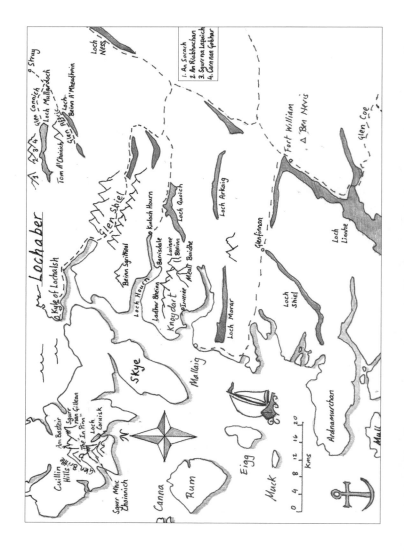

Lochaber

Loch Ness

9 Stray
Glen Cannich
Loch Mullardoch
Beinn A'Mheadhoin
Glen Affric
Tom A'Choinich

1. An Socach
2. An Riabhachan
3. Squrr na Lapaich
4. Càrn nan Gobhar

Fort William
△ Ben Nevis
Glen Coe

Kyle of Lochalsh

Glen Shiel

Beinn Sgritheall
Kinloch Hourn
Loch Quoich

Loch Arkaig

Barrisdale
Luinne Bheinn
Meall Buidhe

Glenfinnan

Loch Hourn

Ladhar Bheinn
Knoydart
Sgurr Mhic Choinnich
Loch Morar

Loch Shiel

Loch Linnhe

Skye

Mallaig

Cuillin Hills
Glen Brittle
An Bàsteir
Sgurr nan Gillean
The In Pinn
Loch Coruisk
Sgurr Mhic Choinnich

Eigg

Ardnamurchan

Mull

Canna

Rum

Muck

0 4 8 12 16 20
Kms

234

21

In the Splendour of His Holiness

Sgurr Mhic Choinnich

I WANT to conclude my own particular exploits in the hills with an outing that stands out above the rest, not that it is a personal favourite by any means as will become clear, but because it is an experience of glimpsing from afar things that are profound.

Sgurr Mhic Choinnich (refer to 'Lochaber' map, p. 234) was to be my nemesis taking three attempts to reach its summit. As mentioned before, each outing brought the frustration of two long round trips up to Skye (involving overnight stays) all carefully planned with time off work and an eye on the weather forecast in the hope of dry conditions without too much wind and high cloud cover, conditions which never seemed to be forecasted whenever the weather websites were browsed. But there are purposes, even in our frustrations:

Hope deferred makes the heart sick
But a longing fulfilled is a tree of life. (Prov. 13:12)

As this peak neighbours the In Pinn, and being termed a technical scramble and very exposed in parts, I had intended to climb this with the guide who took me up the In Pinn, as described in a previous chapter. However, the lengthy wait to scale the In Pinn in tolerable conditions didn't allow time to attempt Sgurr Mhic Choinnich that same day.

My mountain guide had encouraged me to tackle Sgurr Mhic Choinnich on my own, pointing out that I had a certain agility and confidence when scrambling. He also emphasised the desirability of climbing this ridge on a dry day, explaining that the basalt was smooth and very slippery when wet and furthermore it was treacherously set at forty-five degrees. It seemed nature particularly conspired here to make things extremely tricky. I had stayed an extra night after climbing the In Pinn, but with charcoal grey cloud swamping unseen ridges and rain falling abundantly in Glen Brittle, any such thought of tackling the peak evaporated.

The next attempt, a couple of weeks later, promised a small window of dry between rain, the satellite predicting no rain between 5 a.m. and midday. So off I set at the crack of dawn and although it wasn't raining, Coire Laggan was shrouded in shifting mist producing an uneasy kind of twilight, mysteriously darkening the loch at its feet. The arduous toil from the loch to the serrations of Sgurr Mhic Choinnich's ridge was up steep, shifting screes. Drenched in persistent drizzle, the basalt of the summit ridge was wet as could be. As I was up there, I wasn't inclined to turn back, despite the warnings of my guide's words. Encouraged by the initial part of the ridge looking no worse than other places climbed in the Cuillins, I pushed on. Soon the ridge was riven by clefts and sheer chimneys, obstacles around which were faint traces of discolorations on the rock's surface and flattened screes where many climbing boots had scuffed their way along. Along these precipitous tracks absolute concentration was required without a moment's let. The unforgiving gradient and the full extent of the drop hidden by poor visibility, certainly shown to be impressive on the map, gave no pause to my state of heightened agitation. I felt an unnerving disquiet proceeding along this airy narrow corridor suspended over the abyss.

The narrow way

Then came the first main challenge. A narrow gully between rock walls you could touch on either side, leading to a smooth slab facing you that partially jutted out, presenting something of an awkward overhang. Place this obstacle in a playground and you probably wouldn't think anything of scrambling on hands and knees over it. But this was exposed, the wind mocking in gusts and the rock remained slippery. Situated on so very steep a place there would be no stopping a fall, a descent that would go on for hundreds of feet. To the right was a scramble up on to a fin edge of ridge, knife-like and sheer, something you would only edge along on your bum with legs straddling the divide.

For some reason, I failed to see a possible route to the left of the overhanging slab and below a bulging overhang, nor had seen any telltale traces of previous walking parties. I retraced my way back down the narrow gully and there found another goat-like path following the contour along the northern flank of the ridge, a ledge beetling a bold way above a phenomenal drop with a mighty wall rising above. This was such a way that well illustrates this Proverb:

There is a way that seems right to a man,
But in the end it leads to death. (Prov. 16:25)

But quite ignorant, I actually felt pleased to have stumbled on this well-trodden route, glad to have recoiled from daring to edge along the knife-like ridge above. Then the path came to an abrupt end. Assuming the way to be straight up, I began a precarious ascent at first finding conveniently located hand holds which took my mind off the near sheer gradient of this cliff. Maybe it was a question of a few metres scramble that in fair weather wouldn't have seemed so bad had I been able to see the proximity of the ridge top above. Fifteen feet up, the climb became more technical with large amounts of loose material in the rock face. Looking back down to the narrow goat track was unsettling. I began to think of the descent; even if it were possible to gain the summit ridge, one slip would bring sure catastrophe into the mist swirling yawning depths below. As descending is always potentially more treacherous, I cut my losses there and then before the risk increased.

By the time I had inched my way back down to the goat track, I was trembling all over. Every manoeuvre had been so tense that I began to freeze out of absolute fear and only managed to regain semi mobility through prayer. Totally unnerved, I was in no mood to take another look up the narrow gulley.

Defeat is never easy, but I consoled myself at not making a coward's retreat for I had done plenty of 'heroics' for a day and had taken the wise choice to preserve life. When life hangs in a precarious balance, we're reminded that we're not absolute masters of our own destiny. To be overfaced by huge odds can mean that we go thankfully through life without taking things for granted, regarding each day as a gift and thereby living life to the full.

The third and final attempt was a few weeks later when I was down to my final tally of just six Munros. I didn't want this to be my final peak since I had planned my last outing to be something of the long epic taking in several peaks as described at the close of the previous chapter. I had chanced to meet the guide who had led me up the In Pinn in his local pub near Talisker and explained how I had become unnerved. A fellow guide was with him and they looked knowingly at one another, shaking their heads at this false trail and explained where I should have gone.

Now with the detailed knowledge of the route up to the summit, I returned up the narrow gully to the overhanging slab and found the way I had failed to see. But there were further challenges ahead, including the most exposed climbing without rope I've ever tackled. A little fear makes you cautious and wise, but much fear can paralyse! So close to the summit and yet so challenged I did question whether I ought to go on. The final yards were punctuated by long pauses and deep breaths to overcome the stupefying fear. Sometimes it was only prayer that enabled me to overcome the paralysis.

The Lord's mountain

The ascent of the final two hundred feet of Sgurr Mhic Choinnich presented a deeply spiritual experience. Human frailty and mortality were apparent at every step. But more than that, this was hallowed ground where few mortals dare to tread, where the foolhardy would be likely to fall, and the arrogant fail to see the otherworldliness of the experience. Dark spectral columns of rock rose in the eerie shift of white mist confounding any remaining hope of being able to continue. But then some devilish way appeared that I half wished wasn't there, a way across smooth slabs set at steep angles glistening with moisture. I found a finger-tip deep fissure to provide the barest grip while my boots frantically flailed above the chasm; a perilous passage upon the brink, pushing against all the odds. Such becomes the all-consuming quest for the summit; the striving through, the pushing beyond in search of more than just the summit of a peak. The fear, the dismay of not finding the way, the despair of life itself confronts and brings you starkly to face eternity on a journey fraught with lurid images of another world. Then the way is enabled by being so humbled that you pray each step and hand hold of the way, followed by the breakthrough of crawling along the summit ridge in awe of One who is part of this otherworld, who reveals something of the mystery of the splendour of heaven; I knew something of that holy fear of the awesome presence of God, seemingly unapproachable that you are stripped of any remaining boast, in despair of your own salvation and yet aware of a Saviour's will to hold you fast on a line without which there is no hope.

It's a fearful thing to come into His presence, but an experience that brings absolute surrender and a seeking of His will afterwards making us forever march to the beat of a different drum.

Look! The Lord is coming from his dwelling place;
He comes down and treads the high places of the earth.

The mountains melt beneath him and the valleys split
apart,
Like wax before the fire ...
His way is in the whirlwind and the storm, and clouds
are the dust of his feet.
His glory covered the heavens and his praise filled the
earth ...
Plague went before him; pestilence followed his steps.
He stood and shook the earth; he looked and made the
nations tremble.
The ancient mountains crumbled and the age-old hills
collapsed.
As I looked, thrones were set in place, and the Ancient
of Days took his seat.
His clothing was as white as snow; the hair of his head
was white like wool.
His throne was flaming with fire, and its wheels were
all ablaze.
A river of fire was flowing, coming out from before him.
(Micah 1:3-4; Nahum 1:3b; Hab. 3:3,5-6; Dan. 7:9-10)

I would wish Christians to be brought to such a point of being undone, of reaching the end of our resources and understanding through seeing the Lord in the splendour of His holiness. To be overwhelmed by the unsurpassing perfection and otherworldliness of our Lord and be made acutely aware of our own fallenness, as Simon Peter experienced when he realised who this great catcher of fish was in his boat, before whom he fell and when he cried out, 'Go away from me, Lord; I am a sinful man!' (Luke 5:8). Leaders would be stripped of their slick professionalism, services freed from going through the motions, all would be given pause to refrain from repeating the same learned replies, the platitudes that we have been brought up on. If only we could be confronted for just one moment with the greatness of the majesty of our Lord.

Two-sided coin

Some modern worship songs order God to do something, expressing an impertinent familiarity with the King of kings – a title used by the ancient Persians for their ultimate emperor king into whose presence you came with much fear and trembling, who had the power to have you killed immediately. You didn't come into such a king's presence audaciously or presumptuously. The almightiness of our King, the Lord in the splendour of His holiness, is beyond compare. Not that we need fear the Lord as one would some capricious tyrant, but we have lost the sense of holy fear and awe when contemplating God. At least the same reverence ought to be shown the true King that Persians showed their mortal rulers, and naturally our King is infinitely mightier and holier, deserving of far greater reverence. Of course this is just one side of the coin – the awe of the splendour of the Lord's holiness and on the coin's flip side the grace and love of a forgiving Saviour. Sometimes it seems as if today's church has the coin placed down on a tabletop, hiding this awesome face and gazing on the love and forgiveness. Both are vital, but if we are to perceive God correctly we need to pick up this two-sided coin and contemplate one side in the light of the other. Then the grace and the wonder of His love is that much more magnificent in the face of the Holy One to whom all must give account.

Consider the genuine expression that would commend the King to our young people who so often leave unimpressed by the same old church routines and decide to come back no more because the awe and wonder has been replaced with routine. Or of equal concern, if the authentic utterance of praise were to emerge born from such a God-encounter, how it could touch the hearts of those Christians who give up on church where the Spirit of the Lord has departed and all that remains is a formalism that's either deathly dull, or is trumped-up entertainment. What a renewing there would be. We are in dire need of this passionate conviction to blow afresh with the pure oxygen from the heights, to breathe on the dying embers of their hope. And let me define what this 'passionate conviction' is. It's the revelation of God, the Lord in the splendour of His holiness, contrasted by the loving grace of a Saviour who forgives us, that has so impacted us within that demands to express itself and cannot be contained. It has not been whipped up to copy some charismatic evangelist, aping his words, feigning his very expressions, to even stoop to adopt an American accent and idiom that's alien to the setting. Nor is it the passionate expressions to conform to a certain style of so many raised arms and shouted 'Hallelujahs' – that can be a parody and is unlovely when it's not the genuine article. Such expressions can be genuine but when man tries to dictate, to orchestrate a formula, to behave like a shaman interceding between God and the people, then we get in the way of what God's Spirit alone can produce.

The beauty of God's holiness
Some very special times I've witnessed when God's Spirit has been made known among a congregation haven't been at the

243

culmination of some ecstatic praise, or some staccato-like prayer shouted out with unbridled emotion and authority. When God's Spirit comes, there is no missing it – everyone is alert to it. The occasions I recall have been when the congregation is made acutely aware of their fallenness and need. The mood is sombre, quiet, sometimes broken by a muffled sobbing that gathers among the many aware of their own sinfulness. And the glory descends and kisses a guilty world and removes the disgrace and fills us with ineffable joy of being forgiven in the presence of the Holy One who has bought us with His blood. Then there is such oneness felt, oneness with God, oneness with each other that you would only want to linger and to sing His praise and dwell in the shadow of the Almighty. Time is no longer noticed and all would wish that nothing would follow, that life here on earth would be irrevocably caught up and moulded into heaven. That is a foretaste of heaven.

I feel so many Christians have lost contact with the world of God's creation as to be no longer in awe, or to know what that sensation truly is and are therefore incapable of how to express it. Too many are 'wowed' (for I can't use 'awed' in this context) by the latest worship song, the latest 'How to' book, the Bible-study guide that's going to transform our home groups or new evangelistic method devised for this new generation – that they miss the real centre of where our attention and our adoration should be focused. So often what impresses and preoccupies many Christian men are the cutting-edge technologies, the newest app for the latest generation of iPhone and even if this serves some Christian end, it seems that all the enthusiasm and wonder is all spent up here and there's nothing left over. Their eyes have not glimpsed the Almighty One in the splendour of His holiness, who once perceived, abruptly stops us in our tracks, strips us bare and changes us in a twinkling of an eye.

It is gain to come to the end of our own devices and capabilities and be confronted with the truly great things like death suddenly staring us in the face, leading us away from all the petty preoccupations, truly grabbing us by our shirt collars in a stark moment of arrest and reckoning, shaking us with such insistence as to bring us to our senses and to begin to perceive the things that really count, the things of consequence in the context of eternity.

> *But who can endure the day of his coming? Who can stand when he appears? For he will be like a refiner's fire ... He will sit as a refiner and purifier; he will purify ... and refine them like gold and silver. Then the Lord will have men who will bring offerings in righteousness.* (Mal. 3:2-3)

Imagine the expressions of adoration to the King whom we glimpsed in a second of revelation that so opened our eyes! It's that Isaiah moment of seeing 'the Lord seated on a throne, high and exalted', of hearing the adulation of the seraphs' praise, 'calling to one another: "Holy, holy, holy is the Lord Almighty; the whole earth is full of his glory",' which then works such a devastating effect on the prophet that he cries out, 'Woe to me! I am ruined! For I am a man of unclean lips, and I live among a people of unclean lips and my eyes have seen the King, the Lord Almighty.' This produces a symbolic coal that sears his lips from where his own unworthiness found utterance and now his 'guilt is taken away' (Isa. 6:1, 3, 5, 7).

'Then I heard the voice of the Lord saying, "Whom shall I send? And who will go for us?"

And I said, "Here am I. Send me!"' (Isa. 6:8).

Imagine the impact of those authentic words of praise and honour leading to sure convictions that make men and women true followers. Such a testimony would touch the cold indifference of many where faith would be a fervent flame to set the world alight with the passionate conviction of the glory of God in the face of Christ Jesus.

Worship the Lord in the splendour of his holiness;
Tremble before him, all the earth. (Ps. 96:9)

MEDITATION

'In the Splendour of his Holiness'

If you're a hillwalker, or do high adrenaline activities, recall dangerous moments when you've been in fear of your life. If you're not into 'dangerous' activities, bring to mind times when you've been confronted by danger. Can you remember how helpless you felt? How precarious life felt hanging in the balance when everything is stripped away and you're totally dependent upon God.

Read Ezekiel chapter 1. This chapter offers an awesome picture of God a vision that perhaps we can better identify with when we are in a place of danger and we are real in our relating to God, and are not coming with presumptions or impertinent familiarity. Try and create a picture of what Ezekiel describes, at least in your imagination, if not on paper. It's full of mysterious imagery: flashing lightning, molten metal, the four faces of the four creatures, the wheels that are described to be something like gyroscopes? Wheels that are all-seeing. Note the sounds. Imagine the throne set upon a sparkling expanse of ice and the description of the One seated there. This is a vision and we can sense that words are inadequate to describe the absolute awe felt looking at 'the appearance of the likeness of the glory of the Lord'. The vision and summons left Ezekiel exhausted and speechless for seven days. (Ezek. 3:15)

Are you guilty of being so over familiar with God that you presume too much and verge on the impertinent? Are you ever in such awe of God, aware of His pristine holiness and your own unrighteousness that hangs like tattered rags? Have you experienced what Peter felt on realising who it was in his boat who filled the nets with fish and Peter appalled cried out, 'Go away from me, Lord; I am a sinful man!' (Luke 5:8)?

Let John share his vision as we end this meditation. Again picture all the imagery and wonder at their significance. This is the exalted Christ being described and He was obviously someone very fearful to behold for John to swoon as though dead. Note the two-sided coin of the awesome majesty contrasted by the gentleness of the One who stoops to lift us up.

I saw seven golden lampstands, and among the lamp-stands was someone 'like a son of man', dressed in a robe reaching down to his feet and with a golden sash round his chest. His head and hair were white like wool, as white as snow, and his eyes were like blazing fire. His feet were like bronze glowing in a furnace, and his voice was like the sound of rushing waters. In his right hand he held seven stars, and out of his mouth came a sharp double-edged sword. His face was like the sun shining in all its brilliance.

When I saw him, I fell at his feet as though dead. Then he placed his right hand on me and said, 'Do not be afraid. I am the First and the Last. I am the Living One; I was dead, and behold I am alive for ever and ever! And I hold the keys of death and Hades'. (Rev. 1:12-18)

Come let us adore Him.

Creating a Mountainous Panorama of your Life

If you are a picture kind of person, you might find it helpful to create a long mountainous panorama, plotting the life episodes that have been significant for you. To the peaks and valleys can be added the obstacles of lochs and corries to negotiate your way around, or even the forests where for a time we lose sight of where we're going. I have reproduced my own rather naive looking mountainous panorama as an example of what one looks like. It provides a reference point to some key moments shared in this book and a useful summary of the way God has shaped me. This could be a helpful exercise as a spiritual overview of your own spiritual formation, the key moments on your pilgrimage, and reminders of God's faithfulness that will help you trust him in the future.

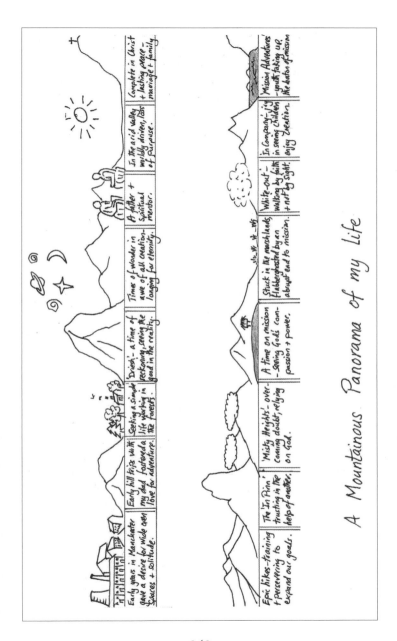

A Mountainous Panorama of my Life

Glossary

Bealach – a mountain pass (from Scots Gaelic in fairly common use).

Belay – to fix a running rope about a fixed object like a rock or a tree.

Ben – a mountain peak (derived from the Gaelic 'Beinn').

Bothy – basic accommodation for rural labourers. Also a term used for a mountain shelter.

Brae – a hillside or a slope.

Breeks – trousers.

Burn – small river, large stream.

Cairn – man-made stone pile used as a marker, found at the summit of any significant hill.

Col – the lowest point on a mountain ridge.

Corrie – a cliff caused by glaciation in mountainous terrain.

Glen – deep valley, narrower than a strath.

Grampian – a mountainous region in the south-east Highlands.

Hebrides – a chain of islands off the west coast of Scotland.

Isthmus – a narrow land bridge, usually across water.

Loch – lake.

Lochan – small lake.

Massif – a large mountainous mass or group of connecting mountains.

Munro – a summit of 3,000 feet or more as listed in the official classification of the Scottish Mountaineering Club originally compiled by Sir Hugh Munro. Some eminences of 3,000 feet are not Munros and are termed as 'tops'. There isn't an exact criterion and the distinction is based on drop in height and distance between neighbouring peaks as well as by their character and the time taken to walk from one to the next. As it's not a definitive science there have been several revisions of the Munro tables where a few former Munros have been demoted and a few new ones added.

Peat hags – plateaus of peat left standing after erosion, forming abrupt sides or free standing stacks.

Peat morass – peat bog.

Piece – refers to a sandwich or snack.

Rubble sack – heavy-duty plastic sack to hold builders' rubble.

Saddle – another term for col, the lowest part of a dip in a ridge that has the cross-sectional appearance of a horse saddle.

Screes – the debris of broken rock at the base of cliffs.

Sheep fanks – an enclosure pen for sheep.

Shielings – stone built huts in high uplands, one-time lived in by families whilst grazing cattle in summer mountain pastures. Can also refer to just the summer pasture.

Steading – a farmstead, often used to refer to its outbuildings.

Stob – a mountain peak (Gaelic).

Strath – a wide valley that is shallow as opposed to a glen that is narrower and steeper.

West Highland Way – long-distance walking route from Milngavie in the north of Glasgow to Fort William.

Scripture References

Chapter No. [ ]

[13] Genesis 12:2-3

[15] Genesis 18:25

[12] Exodus 19:16-19

[7] Joshua 1:6

[17] 1 Samuel 26:21

[15] Job 1:1

[15] Job 1:21

[15] Job 2:5

[15] Job 9:4-12

[19] Job 11:7-9

[19] Job 12:16

[19] Job 19:8

[15] Job 19:25

[18] Job 20:6-9

[19] Job 23:10

[18] Job 24:22-24

[1] Job 26:7-10

[15] Job 38:2-3

[4] Job 38:4-7

[1] Job 38:31-33

[15] Job 40:2

[15] Job 42:3

[1] Psalm 8:3-4

[14] Psalm 18:16-19

[11] Psalm 18:32-33, 35-36

[1] Psalm 19:1-4

[15] Psalm 30:1-5

[16] Psalm 32

[11] Psalm 34:4-6

[11] Psalm 34:7-10

[9] Psalm 40:2, 3

[16] Psalm 42 & 43

[16] Psalm 46

[20] Psalm 51:7, 9, 10, 12

[16] Psalm 73

[4] Psalm 90:2-6

[4] Psalm 90:12

[21] Psalm 96:9

[9] Psalm 96:11-13

[12] Psalm 96:5-6, 9; Psalm 97:2, 4-6 *(Fusion)*

[15] Psalm 102:6-7, 27

[2] Psalm 103:15-16

[12] Psalm 104:1-4

[1] Psalm 108:1-5

[19] Psalm 119:65-72

[13] Psalm 126:5-6

[18] Psalm 130:5-6

[1] Psalm 139:13-16

[5] Psalm 139:14

[2] Proverbs 1:22;

[2] Proverbs 2:1-5

[16] Proverbs 3:5-6

[5] Proverbs 3:13-14, 17-18

[10] Proverbs 3:21-22

[7] Proverbs 3:21-23, 26

[7] Proverbs 4:5-6

[6] Proverbs 4:8-9

[9] Proverbs 4:18

[9] Proverbs 8:22-31

[8] Proverbs 9:6

[21] Proverbs 13:12

[12] Proverbs 16:18

[21] Proverbs 16:25

[17] Proverbs 18:24

[10] Proverbs 19:2

[13] Proverbs 19:21

[7] Proverbs 20:5

[3] Proverbs 22:6

[8] Proverbs 29:25

[1] Ecclesiastes 3:11

[6] Ecclesiastes 4:6

[19] Ecclesiastes 9:11

[21] Isaiah 6:1,3,5,7

[18] Isaiah 40:12

[14] Isaiah 50:4-5

[16] Isaiah 50:10

[4] Jeremiah 10:12-13

[1] Jeremiah 51:15

[21] Ezekiel 1

[21] Ezekiel 3:15

[15] Daniel 4:34-35

[21] Micah 1:3-4; Nahum 1:3b; Habakkuk 3:3, 5-6; Daniel 7:9-10 *(Fusion)*

[8] Amos 4:13

[1] Amos 5:8

[5] Habakkuk 3:19

[21] Malachi 3:2-3

[8] Matthew 5:6,8

[9] Matthew 9:36

[17] Matthew 17:20-21

[17] Matthew 25:21

[13] Matthew 28:18-20

[13] Matthew 28:19

[6] Luke 5:5

[21] Luke 5:8

[8] Luke 15:4-6, 8, 20

[20] Luke 19:1-10

[8] Luke 22:32

[8] Luke 22:61-62

[9] John 1:1-5

[9] John 1:14

[9] John 6:35

[9] John 8:12

[9] John 10:10

[7] John 14:15

[7] John 14:27

[8] John 21:16

[4] Acts 2:13

[9] Acts 2:22, 36, 37-39

[9] Acts 9:13-15

[10] Acts 9:26-27

[10] Acts 11:19-26

[8] Romans 1:20

[11] Romans 5:3-5

[20] Romans 5:3-5

[11] Romans 8:18

[15] Romans 8:28

[16] Romans 12:1-2

[2] Romans 12:2

[16] Romans 12:12

[17] 2 Corinthians 4:16-18

[16] 2 Corinthians 5:7

[15] 2 Corinthians 10:5

[15] Philippians 3:12-14

[13] Colossians 3:2

[2] 1 Timothy 6:6-8

[3] 2 Timothy 1:3-7

[13] 2 Timothy 2:3-4

[17] Hebrews 11:6

[17] Hebrews 12:1

[16] Hebrews 12:1-3

[20] Hebrews 12:10-11

[17] James 5:17

[8] 1 John 1:9

[21] Revelation 1:12-18

[20] Revelation 3:19-20

[14] Revelation 5:9-10

Bibliography

Browning, Robert. *Andrea del Sarto*. From Browning's 1855 poetry collection 'Men and Women'.

Edman, V. Raymond. *Disciplines of Life*. Published in 1948 for the Billy Graham Evangelistic Association by World Wide Publications.

Einstein, Albert. *The World as I See It*. Published in 1956 by Citadel Press, Kensington Publishing Corporation.

FitzGerald, Edward (translated by). *The Rubáiyát of Omar Khayyám*. J. M. Dent & Sons Ltd. First included in Everyman's Library 1954.

Grubb, Norman P. *C.T. Studd: Cricketer and Pioneer*. Published in 1985 by CLC Publications.

Lao-Tzu. *Tao Te Ching*. Published in 1993 by Hackett Publishing Company Inc.

Northumbria Community, From the – *Celtic Daily Prayer*. Published in 2000 by Harper Collins.

Steven, Kenneth C. *Iona Poems*. First published in 2000 by Saint Andrew Press.

Wordsworth, William. *Ode on Immortality*. First published in 1807 in *Poems, in Two Volumes*, Longman, Hurst, Rees and Orme.

Further Reading

Kenneth C. Steven – all the following poem collections
are published by Saint Andrew Press, 121 George
Street, Edinburgh EH2 4YN: *Iona* (2000*); Columba*
(2005), *Salt & Light* (2007).

Smoking the Mango Trees – Martin C. Haworth, published
in 2002 by Monarch Books, Concorde House,
Grenville Place, Mill Hill, London NW7 3SA.

Beyond Coral Shores – Martin C. Haworth, published
in 2006 by Authentic Media, 9 Holdom Avenue,
Bletchley, Milton Keynes, Bucks MK1 1QR.

The Munros edited by Donald Bennet, first published in
1985 by The Scottish Mountaineering Trust.

The Celtic Way – Ian Bradley – published in 2002 by
Darton, Longman & Todd, 1 Spencer Court, 140-142
Wandsworth High Street, London SW18 4JJ.

The Forgotten Faith – Anthony Duncan, first published in
2002 by Sun Chalice Books, Oceanside U.S.A.

Hamish's Mountain Walk – Hamish Brown, published in
1980 by Paladin Books, Granada Publishing Ltd, 8
Grafton Street, London W1X 3LA.

Glory in the Glen

A History of Evangelical Revivals in Scotland 1880-1940

Tom Lennie

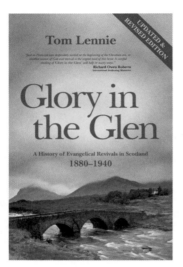

No nation on earth has a richer, more colourful, and more long-standing heritage of evangelical awakenings than Scotland - yet most people are unfamiliar with its dramatic legacy. Most historical studies stop at, or before, the Moody & Sankey Revival of 1873-74. It is commonly assumed that very few genuine revivals occurred since that date until the Lewis Revival of 1949-53. Tom Lennie thoroughly debunks this idea – showing that religious awakenings were relatively common in Scotland between these dates - and provides a comprehensive account of the many exciting revivals that have taken place throughout Scotland. The Awakenings in the Outer Hebrides and North East fishing communities, that had several unique and striking features, are considered in separate sections. Revivals amongst both children / students and Pentecostals are also given separate treatment. Of particular significance is the first comprehensive account of the 1930's 'Laymen's Revival' in Lewis. This fascinating, but near-forgotten, movement may have been even more powerful and influential than the later Lewis Revival. *Glory in the Glen* tells a thoroughly absorbing, and largely untold, story. It is the result of painstaking research, conducted over more than half-a-decade, from hundreds of source materials as well as personal interviews. Much of the material has never before been published.

ISBN 978-1-84550-377-2

Land of Many Revivals

Scotland's Extraordinary LEgacy of Christian Revivals over Four Centuries (1527-1857)

TOM LENNIE

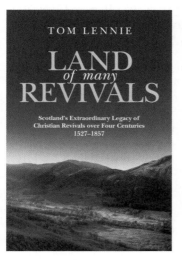

Scotland has arguably the most varied, colourful and longstanding history of evangelical revivals in the world. Focusing on the period between 1527-1857 Tom Lennie provides an illuminating account of many an exciting time. Scotland's true revival legacy is wide and varied and Lennie draws on a variety of sources to bring together this comprehensive resource. *Land of Many Revivals* examines how revival happened in different ways across Scotland and looks at the legacy left in these communities.

...a welcome addition to the literature. It is a wonderful story, and Tom tells it well... May the same divine work which shaped the church in the past continue to come in power to revive us again.

Iain D. Campbell,
Minister
Point Free Church of Scotland, Isle of Lewis

A native of Orkney, Tom Lennie has long held a passion for spiritual revivals worldwide, and owns one of the largest private libraries of revival literature in the UK. He currently resides in Edinburgh, where he is working on the next volume of his trilogy on Scottish revival movements.

ISBN 978-1-78191-520-2

Christian Focus Publications

Our mission statement –

STAYING FAITHFUL
In dependence upon God we seek to impact the world through literature faithful to His infallible Word, the Bible. Our aim is to ensure that the Lord Jesus Christ is presented as the only hope to obtain forgiveness of sin, live a useful life and look forward to heaven with Him.

Our books are published in four imprints:

CHRISTIAN
FOCUS

Popular works including biographies, commentaries, basic doctrine and Christian living.

CHRISTIAN
HERITAGE

Books representing some of the best material from the rich heritage of the church.

MENTOR

Books written at a level suitable for Bible College and seminary students, pastors, and other serious readers. The imprint includes commentaries, doctrinal studies, examination of current issues and church history.

CF4•K

Children's books for quality Bible teaching and for all age groups: Sunday school curriculum, puzzle and activity books; personal and family devotional titles, biographies and inspirational stories – because you are never too young to know Jesus!

Christian Focus Publications Ltd,
Geanies House, Fearn, Ross-shire,
IV20 1TW, Scotland, United Kingdom.
www.christianfocus.com